CO

100
Best-Rated
STOCKS

Neither CONSUMER GUIDE® nor Zacks Investment Research has any connection with any of the firms whose stocks are recommended herein. Nor do either CONSUMER GUIDE® or Zacks Investment Research have any connection with any of the brokerage firms whose ratings provide the basis for the compilations, other than that required of Zacks Investment Research in fulfillment of its roles as information clearinghouse and research vendor.

Zacks Investment Research is a Chicago-based investment consulting firm. Its approach to stock market analysis has been profiled in *The New York Times, The Wall Street Journal, Fortune,* and *Business Week.* Zacks' ratings data is available on *Dow Jones News/Retrieval* and other major electronic distributors.

Compiled by the Editors of CONSUMER GUIDE® and Zacks Investment Research.

CONTENTS

INTRODUCTION

WHAT DOES THIS INFORMATION TELL ME?

100 Best-Rated Stocks is an exclusive, up-to-date overview of the stocks recommended most highly by major brokerage firms. There are more than one hundred such brokerage firms, employing a total of more than 2,500 respected stock analysts. These analysts continually review and analyze the quality of thousands of companies. Their assessments of these companies' prospects become the basis for brokerage house recommendations. These recommendations are then published in brokerage firms' reports and made available to customers through local brokers.

Brokerage ratings are not the final word on stock performance, but they are a major source of investment advice for a great many investors. Zacks Investment Research has been monitoring earnings estimates of brokerage house recommendations since 1978 (available as *EPS* on *Dow Jones News/Retrieval* and elsewhere). Since 1983, Zacks has been monitoring brokerage house stock recommendations as well. Zacks' ratings database, currently covering ratings from well over fifty brokerage houses, is an unparalleled source for a comprehensive consensus of analysts' recommendations regarding more than 3,200 publicly traded stocks. It is thus a natural basis for this CONSUMER GUIDE® *100 Best-Rated Stocks*.

WHAT SORT OF FIRMS' RECOMMENDATIONS ARE SURVEYED?

Most firms can be categorized into one of four areas.
1. **National Retail.** The primary contact for individual investors, these firms have offices in most cities and large (20- to 50-person) research departments. Zacks' database includes all of the major national retail firms, such as E.F. Hutton, Shearson Lehman, and Prudential-Bache.
2. **National Institutional.** These firms specialize in providing high-quality research and trade executions to institutional investors and often have investment banking departments with limited retail sales. Zacks' database includes many of these firms, including Bear Stearns and Kidder Peabody.
3. **Regional Institutional.** Firms such as William Blair and Howard Weil provide high-quality research coverage to companies in their local areas or in special industries. These firms typically have between 5 and 20 analysts. Zacks' database includes most of these firms.
4. **Regional Retail.** Firms such as Mesirow and Interstate Securities serve local interests. Their small (2- to 5-person) research departments may offer specialized coverage of local companies. Zacks' database includes a few of these.

HOW ARE RATINGS CREATED?

Firms in each of the four areas employ stock analysts who usually are specialists in one industry. Each analyst generally identifies the most attractive companies in his or her industry; each firm then compiles a "followed list" made up of the selections of all of their analysts. The followed lists are the starting point for the brokers' ratings. Brokers rate stocks in one of two ways.

1. A committee of senior officers at the firm selects a few companies from the followed list and calls those companies "attractive"; or

2. Each analyst at the firm classifies his or her own stocks into a few groups, such as *buy, hold, moderate sell,* and *sell.* Such terminologies differ widely from firm to firm, but their general intentions are similar.

Zacks has developed a proprietary technique for converting different brokers' ratings terminologies into a uniform 1-to-5 ratings scale. A *1* is the best rating; a *5* is the worst. Based on this method, Zacks calculated Z-Scores for more than 1,500 stocks. The Z-Score is the percent of brokers following the stock who rate it a 1 or a 2. Each stock selected for this publication passed four tests: (1) Each stock was given a rating by at least three brokerage firms; (2) each had an average rating of 1.88 or better; (3) each had a Z-Score of 50.00 or better. For the fourth test, we added a new dimension to our selection process. Stock analysts rate stocks, but before they rate them they generally calculate earnings estimates for the company, that is, assessments of what the firm is likely to earn during various fiscal periods. Since the stocks for this book were selected on the basis of ratings as of July 1987, during a period of almost unprecedented stock market enthusiasm, we eliminated any stocks whose average earnings estimates for the 1988 fiscal year had declined during the past three months. This was done in an attempt to screen out stocks whose ratings were predicated on short-term rationales.

HOW TO READ THIS BOOK

Each stock entry includes:

1. **Company name.**
2. **Listing information:** A parenthetical listing of where the stock is traded, followed by the stock's

ticker symbol. Two major stock exchanges, the New York Stock Exchange (NYSE) and the American Stock Exchange (ASE), are the traditional forums of exchange for securities. The National Association of Securities Dealers' Automated Quotation system (NASDAQ) allows for highly liquid over-the-counter trading of most other publicly traded issues. In the event that the stock has an option (the right to buy or sell the security within a specified time at a fixed price), its option exchange is also listed here.

3. **Type of stock:** Stocks have been classified into a number of categories. The following categories describe the areas of business in which the company may be engaged: Energy and Natural Resources; Industrial Products; Business and Industrial Equipment; Business and Industrial Services; Consumer Goods, durable; Consumer Goods, nondurable; Consumer Services; Retailing; Health Care; and Financial. Another grouping of categories shows aspects of a stock's profile relative to the market. These categories are: Emerging Growth, High Yield, Low P/E Ratio, Low Price, Widely Followed, and Narrowly Followed. The final categories convey additional information useful to the potential investor: Diversified, High Technology, and Foreign.

4. **Z-Score:** This is the percentage of brokers following the stock who rated it a 1.00 (strong buy) or a 2.00 (buy). A Z-Score of 100.00 indicates that all the brokers following the stock rated it a 1.00 or a 2.00. The cut-off for the Zacks selection process was 50.00, or a favorable brokers' consensus of one-half.

5. **Profile:** A summary of what the company does, including per-share earnings for the most recently completed fiscal year, total company revenues, 52-week share-price history, P/E ratio, and indicated regular dividend, as of September 4, 1987. When information is unavailable, N/A (not available) may be shown. When information is irrelevant or mislead-

6   CONSUMER GUIDE®

ing, NMF (nonmeaningful figure) may be shown. Each company's closing share price represents a multiple of its annualized earnings, or a price-to-earnings (P/E) ratio. Since stock purchasers can be said to be buying shares of a company's future earnings, the P/E ratio indicates how highly the market values the company's expected earnings. Although generally the lower the P/E ratio, the lower the real price of the stock, not all low P/E stocks are bargains; some stocks, low priced in earnings terms, are low priced for good reasons. While high P/E evaluations are also sometimes justified, such stocks may be vulnerable to severe price drops in the wake of disappointing earnings events.

6. **Rating:** This lists the number of brokers following the stock, and a breakdown of the individual ratings. A *strong buy* is rated a 1.00; a *buy* is rated a 2.00; a *hold* is rated a 3.00; a *moderate sell* is rated a 4.00; and a *sell* is rated a 5.00. If an individual broker's rating translated into an intermediate score, it would be given the lesser rating; i.e., a 2.50 would be counted here among the holds, as a 3.00 (though the untranslated intermediate rating value would still be used in computing the average rating). The cutoff for our selection was 1.88.

7. **Overview and Perspective:** A brief summary of company activities.

8. **Recent Developments:** Similar to *Overview and Perspective,* but focusing on the near-term view.

9. **Forecast:** Zacks' Consensus is the average of analysts' estimates of the company's expected annual rate of per-share earnings increase over the next five years.

THE INVESTOR'S EDGE

The wise investor will consult further sources before making final market decisions; factual material in this publication has been obtained from sources believed to be reliable but is not guaranteed, and no statement in this book is to be construed as a recommendation to buy or sell securities or to provide investment advice. This publication will, however, provide you with information not easily found elsewhere and may put you on the road to finding promising investment opportunities. The information that you now possess may give you what every stock market investor looks for: an edge.

For further, updated information, write: Zacks Investment Research, 2 North Riverside Plaza, Suite 1600, Chicago, IL 60606; or call (312) 559-9405 for a free sample copy of *Zacks' Analyst Letter* and/or *Zacks' Earnings Forecaster.*

100 BEST-RATED STOCKS

Company Name: ACUSON CORP.
Listing: (OTC) ACSN
Type of Stock: High Technology; Health Care
Z-Score: 60.00
PROFILE: Acuson is a manufacturer of diagnostic imaging systems, with 1986 per-share earnings of $0.39 on total 1986 revenues of $64 million. As of September 4, 1987, the range of ACSN's price during the previous twelve months was:
• High: $23^1/_4$ • Low: $7^1/_2$
ACSN's price as of the close of the first week in September was $21^7/_8$.
• P/E ratio: 38   • Dividend: None
RATING: Of the five brokers following ACSN, three rate it a strong buy and two rate it a hold. The average of the brokers' ratings is 1.80.
OVERVIEW AND PERSPECTIVE: Founded in 1981, California-based ACSN designs, produces, and sells advanced-technology ultrasound imaging systems for medical diagnostic purposes. ACSN is recognized as a market leader in the ultrasonic imaging field.
RECENT DEVELOPMENTS: Earnings for the first half of 1987, $0.30, were up 131 percent from the $0.13 ACSN posted for the comparable 1986 period. Analysts expect ACSN earnings to grow significantly over the near-term: $0.61 for 1987 and $0.86

for 1988, versus $0.39 in 1986, which are increases of 56 percent and 41 percent, respectively. These figures suggest that, in the near term, ACSN's growth could top the 34-percent rate.

FORECAST: Zacks' Consensus forecasts a 34.00 percent average annual earnings-per-share increase over the next five years.

Company Name: **ADVANCE CIRCUITS, INC.**
Listing: **(NASDAQ) ADVC**
Type of Stock: **High Technology; Industrial Products; Low Price**
Z-Score: **100.00**

PROFILE: Advance Circuits, Inc. is the leading independent supplier of specialized printed circuits for commercial and military markets, with a fiscal August 1986 per-share loss of –$0.78 on total revenues of $55.4 million. As of September 4, 1987, the range of ADVC's price during the previous twelve months was:

• High: $7^{1}/_{2}$ • Low: 2

ADVC's price as of the close of the first week in September was $5^{1}/_{4}$.

• P/E ratio: 25   • Dividend: None

RATING: Of the four brokers following ADVC, one rates it a strong buy and three rate it a buy. The average of the brokers' ratings is 1.70.

OVERVIEW AND PERSPECTIVE: This long-time supplier of state-of-the-art printed circuits for military applications adopted a strategy in 1979 to extend its expertise into the commercial aerospace market. As a result of acquisitions and internal growth, such sales have exceeded 50 percent of total revenues in each of the past three fiscal years. Despite this achievement, financial results in fiscal 1986 reflected severe price competition in the commercial electronics industry resulting from slack demand from electronics manufacturers.

RECENT DEVELOPMENTS: Thanks to the continuing recovery of demand for electronic components in general and the company's specialized products in particular, ADVC reported a third-quarter (May 1987) profit of 8 cents a share on sales of $19.4 million, compared to 3 cents on sales of $15.6 million in the year-earlier period.

FORECAST: Zacks' Consensus forecasts a 16.33 percent average annual earnings-per-share increase over the next five years.

Company Name: **ALBERTO-CULVER COMPANY**
(class B shares)
Listing: **(NYSE) ACV**
Type of Stock: **Consumer Goods, nondurable**
Z-Score: **80.00**

PROFILE: Alberto-Culver Company is one of the largest diversified manufacturers of brand-name consumer products in the U.S., with fiscal September 1986 per-share earnings of $1.04 on total revenues of $435 million. As of September 4, 1987, the range of ACV's price during the previous twelve months was:
• High: 24   • Low: $13^1/_2$
ACV's price as of the close of the first week in September was 21.
• P/E ratio: 18   • Dividend: $0.24

RATING: Of the five brokers following ACV, three rate it a strong buy, one rates it a buy, and one rates it a hold. The average of the brokers' ratings is 1.50.

OVERVIEW AND PERSPECTIVE: Originally a long-time supplier of hair care products (Alberto VO5), Alberto-Culver initiated a series of acquisitions over the years to diversify into related consumer products to which its marketing and distribution skills could be applied. These included toiletries, grocery and household products, wholesale beauty supplies, and institutional food and maintenance services.

RECENT DEVELOPMENTS: ACV's interest in further diversifying its product offerings prompted its unsuccessful July 1987 tender offer for Lamaur Inc., a respected manufacturer of hair care and personal grooming products. As of September 1987, Lamaur had managed to forestall ACV's attempted takeover.

FORECAST: Zacks' Consensus forecasts a 15.50 percent average annual earnings-per-share increase over the next five years.

Company Name: **AMERICAN MANAGEMENT SYSTEMS, INC.**

Listing: **(NASDAQ) AMSY**
Type of Stock: **Business and Industrial Services**
Z-Score: 83.33

PROFILE: American Management Systems, Inc. is one of the largest suppliers of computer services in the U.S., with 1986 per-share earnings of $0.51 on total revenues of $135 million. As of September 4, 1987, the range of AMSY's price during the previous twelve months was:

• High: $19^{1}/_{4}$ • Low: $6^{5}/_{8}$

AMSY's price as of the close of the first week in September was $17^{3}/_{8}$.

• P/E ratio: 32   • Dividend: None

RATING: Of the six brokers following AMSY, two rate it a strong buy, three rate it a buy, and one rates it a hold. The average of the brokers' ratings is 1.83.

OVERVIEW AND PERSPECTIVE: Revenues of this 17-year-old computer services and consulting company have increased annually because of management efforts to focus on five target markets. In the order of contribution to sales, they are: federal government agencies and aerospace companies; financial services institutions; state and local government, school districts, and universities; energy companies; and telecommunications firms. Miscellaneous clients, a sixth category, covers a wide range of customers and activities.

RECENT DEVELOPMENTS: 1986 saw AMSY's introduction of two major applications for the financial services field, where AMSY's marketing has to date resulted in its gaining 38 of the country's top 50 banks as clients. AMSY reported that earnings for the second quarter, which ended June 30, 1987, reached 13 cents a share, compared to 11 cents for the year-earlier period, and that revenues advanced to $41.0 million, compared to $32.8 million previously.

FORECAST: Zacks' Consensus forecasts a 26.00 percent average annual earnings-per-share increase over the next five years.

Company Name: **AMERICAN PRESIDENT COMPANIES, LTD.**
Listing: **(NYSE) APS (Options on PAC)**
Type of Stock: **Business and Industrial Services**
Z-Score: **83.33**

PROFILE: American President Companies, Ltd. is an integrated container, transportation, and distribution-services company operating in international and domestic markets, with 1986 per-share earnings of $0.71 on total revenues of $1.47 million. As of September 4, 1987, the range of APS's price during the previous twelve months was:
• High: 51   • Low: 23⅝
APS's price as of the close of the first week in September was 45¼.
• P/E ratio: 17   • Dividend: $0.50

RATING: Of the six brokers following APS, two rate it a strong buy, three rate it a buy, and one rates it a hold. The average of the brokers' ratings is 1.83.

OVERVIEW AND PERSPECTIVE: With origins dating back to 1848, APS has been a major participant in the Pacific shipping business. In 1977, the company enhanced its market position by acquiring domestic truck and rail transportation services to link with the international cargo business. In recent years, APS has strengthened its domestic rail haul service by utilizing double-stacked rail cars and acquiring a major freight forwarding operation. APS was able to retain profitability and maximize capacity utilization during volatile shipping rate wars in 1984 and 1985.

RECENT DEVELOPMENTS: APS will be enlarging its fleet with "jumbo ships," which offer economies of scale APS thinks likely to outweigh possible problems involving the adaptation of existing port facilities to the larger vessels. In its domestic operation, APS has exceeded the industry average for rail capacity and maintains a competitive edge in the transport of time-sensitive cargo.

FORECAST: Zacks' Consensus forecasts a 12.75 percent average annual earnings-per-share increase over the next five years.

Company Name: **AMERICAN TELEVISION & COMMUNICATIONS CORP.**

Listing: (NASDAQ) ATCMA

Type of Stock: **Business and Industrial Services; Consumer Services**

Z-Score: **83.33**

PROFILE: American Television & Communications Corp. is a cable television systems operator, with 1986 per-share earnings of $0.37 (total revenues not available). As of September 4, 1987, the range of ATCMA's price during the previous twelve months was:

• High: 29⅝   • Low: 14½

ATCMA's price as of the close of the first week in September was 28⅛.

• P/E ratio: 108   • Dividend: None

RATING: Of the six brokers following ATCMA, four rate it a strong buy, one rates it a buy, and one rates it a hold. The average of the brokers' ratings is 1.50.

OVERVIEW AND PERSPECTIVE: Effectively a subsidiary of media/publishing giant Time Inc., ATCMA is a rapidly growing presence in the cable television industry. Founded in 1968, it now runs cable franchises all across North America. Less than a year after Time offered a minority interest in ATCMA to the public in 1986, it transferred ownership of its Manhattan Cable Television system to ATCMA.

RECENT DEVELOPMENTS: In 1987, ATCMA agreed to carry C.O.M.B.'s Cable Value Network on its systems for seven years. ATCMA was also said to have been among bidders for Storer Cable, the fourth-largest cable operator in the country.

FORECAST: Zacks' Consensus forecasts a 42.00 percent average annual earnings-per-share increase over the next five years.

Company Name: **ANCHOR GLASS CONTAINER CORPORATION**

Listing: **(NYSE) ANC**

Type of Stock: **Industrial Products**

Z-Score: **85.71**

PROFILE: Anchor Glass Container Corporation is a leading manufacturer of glass containers serving the food, beverage, and cosmetic industries, with 1986 per-share earnings of $1.71 on total revenues of $587 million. As of September 4, 1987, the range of ANC's price during the previous twelve months was:

- High: 30$^{1}/_{2}$ • Low: 10$^{3}/_{8}$

ANC's price as of the close of the first week in September was 22$^{3}/_{4}$.

- P/E ratio: 14   • Dividend: $0.08

RATING: Of the seven brokers following ANC, three rate it a strong buy, three rate it a buy, and one rates it a hold. The average of the brokers' ratings is 1.64.

OVERVIEW AND PERSPECTIVE: Anchor, the third-largest U.S. manufacturer in the glass container industry, was formed in 1983 as a result of a leveraged buyout of the Glass Container Division of the Anchor Hocking Corporation. The following year Anchor acquired the Midland Glass Company, significantly enhancing Anchor's size and market penetration. The company's initial public offering of common stock in June 1986 generated $28.6 million in proceeds for Anchor. Recent capital spending has resulted in the purchase of state-of-the-art technology for production lines. Anchor, headquartered in Tampa, Florida, operates twelve manufacturing plants in ten states.

RECENT DEVELOPMENTS: In June of 1987, Anchor began its acquisition of Diamond-Bathurst Inc., a company with major markets closely aligned to Anchor's.

FORECAST: Zacks' Consensus forecasts an 11.00 percent average annual earnings-per-share increase over the next five years.

Company Name: **ARISTECH CHEMICAL CORP.**
Listing: **(NYSE) ARS**
Type of Stock: **Industrial Products; Narrowly Followed**
Z-Score: **66.67**

PROFILE: Aristech Chemical Corp. is a manufacturer of polymer products and other chemicals, with 1986 per-share earnings of $1.70 on total revenues of $751 million. As of September 4, 1987, the range of ARS's price during the previous twelve months was:
- High: $38^{1}/_{2}$ • Low: $17^{3}/_{4}$

ARS's price as of the close of the first week in September was 35.

- P/E ratio: 18   • Dividend: $0.36

RATING: Of the three brokers following ARS, two rate it a strong buy and one rates it a hold. The average of the brokers' ratings is 1.67.

OVERVIEW AND PERSPECTIVE: Prior to its initial public offering in 1986, ARS was the USS Chemicals division of USX Corp. ARS's sales are divided evenly between polymers and related products and other chemicals. A major force in the production of polyester and polypropylene resins, ARS plans to bolster capital spending and is considering several strategic acquisitions that will enable it to offer a wider range of new products.

RECENT DEVELOPMENTS: ARS sold an olefin plant in Texas in 1987 but indicated that production capacity for polypropylene, phenol, and bisphenol products would be increased.

FORECAST: Zacks' Consensus forecasts a 25.00 percent average annual earnings-per-share increase over the next five years.

Company Name: **ATLANTIC SOUTHEAST AIRLINES, INC.**

Listing: (OTC) ASAI

Type of Stock: **Consumer Services; Business and Industrial Services**

Z-Score: **66.67**

PROFILE: Atlantic Southeast Airlines, Inc. is the largest regional airline in the Southeast, with 1986 per-share earnings of $0.87 on total revenues of $92.3 million. As of September 4, 1987, the range of ASAI's price during the previous 12 months was:

- High: 13¾   • Low: 9⅜

ASAI's price as of the close of the first week in September was 12¾.

- P/E ratio: 14   • Dividend: None

RATING: Of the six brokers following ASAI, three rate it as a strong buy, one rates it a buy, and two rate it a hold. The average of the brokers' ratings is 1.83.

OVERVIEW AND PERSPECTIVE: Starting in Atlanta with one aircraft in 1979, ASAI has expanded to become the southeast region's largest air carrier. This position was enhanced with the "Delta Connection," a program with Delta Airlines in which Atlantic's flights are given a priority listing in reservation terminals for connecting flights with that carrier. In 1986, Delta purchased newly issued common stock from the company, which gave it a 20 percent ownership in ASAI.

RECENT DEVELOPMENTS: The company said its revenue passenger miles flown for the first six months of the year were up 23.7 percent from the like period a year earlier.

FORECAST: Zacks' Consensus forecasts a 15.75 percent average annual earnings-per-share increase over the next five years.

Company Name: AVEMCO CORPORATION
Listing: (NYSE) AVE
Type of Stock: Financial; Business and Industrial
                          Services; Low P/E
Z-Score: 66.67

PROFILE: AVEMCO Corporation is a major writer of aviation insurance, with 1986 per-share earnings of $1.13 on total revenues of $95.3 million. As of September 4, 1987, the range of AVE's price during the previous twelve months was:
- High: 25$\frac{1}{4}$ • Low: 12$\frac{1}{2}$

AVE's price as of the close of the first week in September was 21$\frac{1}{2}$.
- P/E ratio: 12   • Dividend: $0.28

RATING: Of the six brokers following AVE, three rate it a strong buy, one rates it a buy, and two rate it a hold. The average of the brokers' ratings is 1.83.

OVERVIEW AND PERSPECTIVE: AVE, founded in 1959, continues to be the world's major underwriter of insurance for aviation but in recent years has been branching into related areas. Aviation-related reinsurance, marine insurance, medical assistance services, and insurance products for financial institutions are markets in which AVE sees opportunity for leveraging its aviation-insurance market presence and experience.

RECENT DEVELOPMENTS: During 1987, AVE's financial marketing subsidiary, Matterhorn Bank Programs, saw a 46 percent increase in premiums over the comparable 1986 period, suggesting strong growth potential for insuring bank loans on such big-ticket purchases as automobiles, aircraft, and pleasure boats.

FORECAST: Zacks' Consensus forecasts a 17.38 percent average annual earnings-per-share increase over the next five years.

Company Name: **AVERY INTERNATIONAL**
Listing: **(NYSE) AVY**
Type of Stock: **Industrial Products; Consumer Goods, nondurable**
Z-Score: **80.00**

PROFILE: Avery International is a leading worldwide manufacturer of self-adhesive labels, retail tags, and price-marking equipment, with 1986 per-share earnings of $1.23 on total revenues of $1.13 billion. As of September 4, 1987, the range of AVY's price during the previous twelve months was:
* High: 29$\frac{1}{4}$ * Low: 18$\frac{1}{8}$
AVY's price as of the close of the first week in September was 26$\frac{1}{4}$.

- P/E ratio: 20   • Dividend: $0.42

RATING: Of the ten brokers following AVY, three rate it a strong buy, five rate it a buy, and two rate it a hold. The average of the brokers' ratings is 1.88.

OVERVIEW AND PERSPECTIVE: Though perhaps best known for its prominently marketed consumer and office products, notably labels, AVY moved into its second half-century with an enviable degree of product-line diversity. AVY manufactures retail tags, adhesives, computer products, and pressure-sensitive specialty-adhesive graphic materials, and has successfully marketed these products to customers around the world.

RECENT DEVELOPMENTS: AVY's adhesives group has been finding new applications in medical products (including medical adhesive tape whose transparency greatly simplifies the monitoring of treatment areas) and electronics. AVY is also using its long-time presence in office-supply and stationery stores to good advantage in competing for a piece of the semiadhesive-notepad market.

FORECAST: Zacks' Consensus forecasts a 13.22 percent average annual earnings-per-share increase over the next five years.

Company Name: **BANCTEC**
Listing: **(NASDAQ) BTEC**
Type of Stock: **Business and Industrial Equipment; Narrowly Followed; Low Price**
Z-Score: 66.67

PROFILE: BancTec develops equipment and systems for automated document processing, with fiscal March 1987 per-share earnings of $0.71 on total revenues of $370 million. As of September 4, 1987, the range of BTEC's price during the previous twelve months was:
- High: 15$7/8$ • Low: 5$3/4$

BTEC's price as of the close of the first week in September was 11 3/4.

• P/E ratio: 14   • Dividend: None

RATING: Of the three brokers following BTEC, two rate it a strong buy and one rates it a hold. The average of the brokers' ratings is 1.50.

OVERVIEW AND PERSPECTIVE: BTEC's product lines rapidly process a variety of business documents, including checks, sales drafts, and payment stubs. These products are sold to end-users, original equipment manufacturers (OEM), and the value-added reseller markets (VAR). In the early 1980s, nearly all of BTEC's principal customers were in banking, but since deregulation has resulted in a broader range of competitors in the financial services field, BTEC has seen a parallel expansion of its customer base. In 1986, 40 percent of end-user sales came from industries other than banking. Research and product expansion has resulted in a new-generation check reader/sorter, and enhanced-image capture capabilities and encoder technology.

RECENT DEVELOPMENTS: BTEC's subsidiary (BTI Systems) has a new contract with Honeywell for developing a second-generation high-speed page printer system. Targeted reorganization has contributed to cost reductions in manufacturing and improved turnaround for customer support services.

FORECAST: Zacks' Consensus forecasts a 15.00 percent average annual earnings-per-share increase over the next five years.

Company Name: **BANK OF BOSTON CORP.**
Listing: **(NYSE) BKB**
Type of Stock: **Financial; Widely Followed; High Yield**
Z-Score: 60.00

PROFILE: Bank of Boston Corp. is the holding company for the largest bank in New England, with

1986 per-share earnings of $3.69 on total revenues of $3.54 billion. As of September 4, 1987, the range of BKB's price during the previous twelve months was:
• High: 38 • Low: 24¼
BKB's price as of the close of the first week in September was 32⅝.
• P/E ratio: 18 • Dividend: $1.00

RATING: Of the fifteen brokers following BKB, seven rate it a strong buy, two rate it a buy, and six rate it a hold. The average of the brokers' ratings is 1.87.

OVERVIEW AND PERSPECTIVE: BKB owns the Bank of Boston, a large money-center bank with more than a hundred offices around the world. BKB has focused on regional and wholesale banking, leveraging strengths gained in decades of commercial banking to win a strategic niche in the rapidly changing financial services environment. Real estate finance, factoring, and other noncredit services stand to play a large role.

RECENT DEVELOPMENTS: Acquisitions in 1987 included a Florida trust company, savings bank properties in New England, and participations in Korea and the Philippines.

FORECAST: Zacks' Consensus forecasts a 10.58 percent average annual earnings-per-share increase over the next five years.

Company Name: **BAY VIEW FEDERAL SAVINGS & LOAN ASSOCIATION**
Listing: **(NASDAQ) BVFS**
Type of Stock: **Financial; Low P/E**
Z-Score: **100.00**

PROFILE: Bay View Federal Savings & Loan Association is a San Mateo (California)-based thrift institution, with 1986 per-share earnings of $2.53 on total revenues of $162 million. As of September 4, 1987, the range of BVFS's price during the previous twelve months was:

- High: $18^3/_4$
- Low: $11^5/_8$

BVFS's price as of the close of the first week in September was $17^7/_8$.

- P/E ratio: 7
- Dividend: None

RATING: Of the five brokers following BVFS, two rate it a strong buy and three rate it a buy. The average of the brokers' ratings is 1.46.

OVERVIEW AND PERSPECTIVE: A mutual (owned by its accountholders) savings institution until it converted to stock-form ownership in May 1986, BVFS is a fast-growing S&L benefiting from several positive trends in the San Francisco area—among these a consistently strong real estate market.

RECENT DEVELOPMENTS: Heavy promotion of adjustable-rate mortgages (ARMs) by the three largest California thrifts—Ahmanson, Golden West, and Great Western—has accrued to BVFS's advantage. Roughly 60 percent of its outstanding mortgages are ARMs, giving it an enviable degree of insulation from interest-rate volatility.

FORECAST: Zacks' Consensus forecasts a 9.00 percent average annual earnings-per-share increase over the next five years.

Company Name: **BDM INTERNATIONAL, INC.**
Listing: **(ASE) BDM**
Type of Stock: **Business and Industrial Services; High Technology**
Z-Score: 62.50

PROFILE: BDM International, Inc. provides specialized technical and professional services to defense, space, communications, business, and energy companies, with 1986 per-share earnings of $1.21 on total revenues of $322 million. As of September 4,

1987, the range of BDM's price during the previous twelve months was:

- High: 35¾
- Low: 22½

BDM's price as of the close of the first week in September was 34¼.

- P/E ratio: 24
- Dividend: $0.14

RATING: Of the eight brokers following BDM International, four rate it a strong buy, one rates it a buy, and three rate it a hold. The average of the brokers' ratings is 1.79.

OVERVIEW AND PERSPECTIVE: Primarily a defense contractor, BDM has snared Pentagon contracts for projects that range from "ultra-capacitors" for space applications to computerized wargame simulation systems. Management's strategy over the twenty-six years it has been in business is to seek new contracts that promise to be ongoing and lead to additional awards that will draw on its expertise.

RECENT DEVELOPMENTS: BDM was recently awarded an $8 million U.S. Air Force contract for medical research support, which will further add to the company's overall record backlog to be performed in the future.

FORECAST: Zacks' Consensus forecasts a 20.83 percent average annual earnings-per-share increase over the next five years.

Company Name: **BIOMET, INC.**
Listing: **(NASDAQ) BMET**
Type of Stock: **Health Care; Emerging Growth**
Z-Score: **77.77**

PROFILE: Biomet, Inc. produces surgical implants and orthopedic support devices, with fiscal May 1987 per-share earnings of $0.69 on total revenues of $55.9 million. As of September 4, 1987, the range of BMET's price during the previous twelve months was:

• High: 28½   • Low: 13⅜

BMET's price as of the close of the first week in September was 27½.

• P/E ratio: 40   • Dividend: None

RATING: Of the nine brokers following BMET, five rate it a strong buy, two rate it a buy, and two rate it a hold. The average of the brokers' ratings is 1.67.

OVERVIEW AND PERSPECTIVE: BMET's products are used by orthopedic medical specialists in the replacement of and support for hip and knee joints as well as in healing fractures. Reconstructive devices have accounted for most of the company's sales, but the late fiscal 1984-85 acquisition of a line of orthopedic supplies, implants, and related products broadened its revenues and earnings base this past period.

RECENT DEVELOPMENTS: In April 1987, BMET and International Genetic Engineering joined forces in developing protein products for the enhancement of bone and cartilage formation. BMET's $4.5 million financing commitment not only entitles it to a 50 percent share in any profits but also gives it exclusive rights to market orthopedic products resulting from the endeavor.

FORECAST: Zack's Consensus forecasts a 27.33 percent average annual earnings-per-share increase over the next five years.

Company Name: **BRISTOL-MYERS**

Listing: **(NYSE) BMY (Options on CBOE)**

Type of Stock: **Widely Followed; Health Care; Consumer Goods, nondurable**

Z-Score: 68.97

PROFILE: Bristol-Myers is a large, diversified manufacturer of health and household products, with 1986 per-share earnings of $2.11 on total revenues of $4.84 billion. As of September 4, 1987, the range of BMY's price during the previous twelve months was:

- High: 55³/₄ • Low: 33⁵/₈

BMY's price as of the close of the first week in September was 49¹/₂.

- P/E ratio: 22 • Dividend: $1.40

RATING: Of the twenty-nine brokers following BMY, thirteen rate it a strong buy, seven rate it a buy, and nine rate it a hold. The average of the brokers' ratings is 1.83.

OVERVIEW AND PERSPECTIVE: Strong positions in proprietary drugs, such as a leading anticancer agent, Platinol, and a variety of nondrug consumer products (including Ban, Bufferin, and Clairol), as well as such household products as Windex and Drano, continue to make good for the New York-based manufacturer. BMY, which recently celebrated its centennial in the drug and consumer-goods business, is positioning itself to help meet a predicted threefold increase in world demand for pharmaceuticals over the next thirteen years. Currently the company has leading positions in anticancer agents, antibiotics, medical implants, nutritional products, and treatments for central nervous system ailments and cardiovascular disease.

RECENT DEVELOPMENTS: The FDA, in its approval of BMY's anxiety ameliorant BuSpar, was sufficiently impressed by its innocuousness (studies suggest minimal potential for abuse or addiction) to refrain from classifying it as a controlled substance; doctors have been similarly appreciative in prescribing it to patients. BMY also finalized a joint marketing agreement with SmithKline Beckman in 1987 and continued research on the development of an AIDS vaccine.

FORECAST: Zacks' Consensus forecasts a 14.20 percent average annual earnings-per-share increase over the next five years.

Company Name: **BROCKWAY, INC.**
Listing: (NYSE) BRK
Type of Stock: **Industrial Products; Consumer Services; Diversified**
Z-Score: **100.00**

PROFILE: Brockway, Inc. produces glass, plastic, and metal containers and operates three regional airlines, with 1986 per-share earnings of $2.44 on total revenues of $1.07 billion. As of September 4, 1987, the range of BRK's price during the previous twelve months was:

• High: 48¼   • Low: 22

BRK's price as of the close of the first week in September was 38⅞.

• P/E ratio: 14   • Dividend: $0.96

RATING: Of the four brokers following BRK, two rate it a strong buy and two rate it a buy. The average of the brokers' ratings is 1.50.

OVERVIEW AND PERSPECTIVE: Formerly Brockway Glass, BRK is a major producer of glass containers. Diversification into plastic and metal containers now accounts for 40 percent of total revenues. Airline operations consist of commuter service centered in Pittsburgh, New York City, Washington, D.C., and New England.

RECENT DEVELOPMENTS: A moderate resurgence in demand for glass bottles (after a continuing loss of market share to plastic containers), combined with the upgrading of BRK's bottle-making facilities, bodes well for improved margins in the main area of its business. Sharp sales increases were posted in 1986 by the company's "captainer" division, which makes molded plastic-lidded containers with offset-quality graphics. In September 1987, Owens-Illinois made a $60-per-share offer for BRK.

FORECAST: Zacks' Consensus forecasts an 11.75 percent average annual earnings-per-share increase over the next five years.

Company Name: **CASTLE & COOKE, INC.**
Listing: **(NYSE) CKE (Options on PAC)**
Type of Stock: **Consumer Goods, nondurable;**
Business and Industrial Services;
Diversified
Z-Score: **80.00**

PROFILE: Castle & Cooke, Inc. is a major food processor and distributor, with interests in transportation and real estate, with 1986 per-share earnings of $1.34 on total revenues of $1.74 billion. As of September 4, 1987, CKE's price during the previous twelve months was:

• High: $26^5/_8$　　　　• Low: $16^1/_8$

CKE's price as of the close of the first week in September was $24^1/_2$.

• P/E ratio: 42　　　　• Dividend: None

RATING: Of the five brokers following CKE, two rate it a strong buy, two rate it a buy, and one rates it a hold. The average of the brokers' ratings is 1.66.

OVERVIEW AND PERSPECTIVE: CKE is the world's largest producer of fresh and processed pineapple and the second largest producer of bananas, under the Dole brand name. Other subsidiary interests include real estate development and transportation-equipment leasing. An ostensible 1985 merger with Flexi-Van (Flexi-Van, headed by financier David Murdock, effectively bought CKE) resulted in a corporate reorganization as a holding company with three divisions: Dole Food, Flexi-Van Leasing, and Oceanic Properties.

RECENT DEVELOPMENTS: July 1987 saw CKE file for yet another restructuring, this one involving the spinoff of what remains of Flexi-Van (CKE had sold its container fleet earlier in the year) to CKE's shareholders, via a rights distribution. Given David Murdock's interest in maximizing shareholder value, further development of the Dole product line (with emphasis on more value-added convenience products) and CKE's vast Hawaiian real estate holdings may be in the works.

FORECAST: Zacks' Consensus forecasts a 20.00 percent average annual earnings-per-share increase over the next five years.

Company Name: **CHEMFIX TECHNOLOGIES**
Listing: **(NASDAQ) CFIX**
Type of Stock: **Business and Industrial Services;**
                Narrowly Followed; Low Price
Z-Score: **66.67**

PROFILE: Chemfix Technologies, a firm that provides chemical waste services, had fiscal August 1986 per-share losses of –$0.12 on total revenues of $4.6 million. As of September 4, 1987, the range of CFIX's price during the previous twelve months was:
• High: $9^{1}/_{4}$ • Low: $5^{1}/_{4}$
CFIX's price as of the close of the first week in September was $7^{5}/_{8}$.
• P/E ratio: N/A   • Dividend: None

RATING: Of the three brokers following CFIX, one rates it a strong buy, one rates it a buy, and one rates it a hold. The average of the brokers' ratings is 1.83.

OVERVIEW AND PERSPECTIVE: CFIX engages in a variety of waste-treatment and environmental services on behalf of both industrial and municipal clients. Its proprietary Chemfix process renders toxic wastes innocuous, at least from an environmental-impact standpoint, thus making possible their further use or disposal. CFIX licenses its process to firms overseas.

RECENT DEVELOPMENTS: In 1986, CFIX received an $8 million contract for waste processing at an Amoco refinery in Illinois. In 1987, the company undertook a research contract in conjunction with the Massachusetts Water Resource Authority.

FORECAST: Zacks' Consensus forecasts a 42.50 percent average annual earnings-per-share increase over the next five years.

Company Name: **CIRCUIT CITY STORES**
Listing: **(NYSE) CC (Options on PAC)**
Type of Stock: **Retailing**
Z-Score: **90.00**

PROFILE: Circuit City Stores is a specialty retailer of consumer electronics products, with fiscal 1986 (ended February 1987) per-share earnings of $1.58 on total revenues of $1.01 billion. As of September 4, 1987, the range of CC's price during the previous twelve months was:

• High: 41⅝   • Low: 20¼

CC's price as of the close of the first week in September was 35¾.

• P/E ratio: 21   • Dividend: $0.08

RATING: Of the ten brokers following CC, seven rate it a strong buy, two rate it a buy, and one rates it a hold. The average of the brokers' ratings is 1.40.

OVERVIEW AND PERSPECTIVE: CC sells audio and video equipment, consumer electronics goods, and appliances through retail stores in the Southeast and California. CC's "Superstores," classic "category-killer" warehouse outlets, offer shoppers the best of both price and selection.

RECENT DEVELOPMENTS: CC's expansion plans call for the opening of as many as two dozen new stores a year, most within a day's drive of existing warehouse facilities. The company's impressive entry into the Los Angeles market a few years ago has set the stage for a move north to the San Francisco area.

FORECAST: Zacks' Consensus forecasts a 24.50 percent average annual earnings-per-share increase over the next five years.

Company Name: **CITIZENS UTILITIES
COMPANY (class A)**
Listing: **(NASDAQ) CITUA**
Type of Stock: **Energy and Natural Resources;
Business and Industrial Services;
Consumer Services; Narrowly
Followed**
Z-Score: **100.00**

PROFILE: Citizens Utilities Company operates
through divisions that supply electric, gas, tele-
phone, water, or wastewater services to customers in
ten states, with 1986 per-share earnings of $1.36 on
total operating revenues of $268 million. As of Sep-
tember 4, 1987, the range of CITUA's price during
the previous twelve months was:
• High: 36¼   • Low: 21¾
CITUA's price as of the close of the first week in September was 36.
• P/E ratio: 25   • Dividend: NMF

RATING: Of the three brokers following CITUA,
two rate it as a strong buy and one rates it as a buy.
The average of the brokers' ratings is 1.33.

OVERVIEW AND PERSPECTIVE: CITUA's operations are diversified, in services—40 percent tele-
phone, 38 percent electric, 16 percent water and
wastewater, and 4 percent gas—and in areas covered:
Arizona, California, Colorado, Hawaii, Idaho, Illinois, Indiana, Ohio, Pennsylvania, and Vermont. Citizens Utilities' investor-oriented stock structure is
unusual: dividends, paid in stock, are not taxed at
time of receipt, although in the event of their sale,
shareholders will have capital gains tax liability for
these shares, based on the difference between sale
price and their "adjusted basis" purchase price.
Cash-insistent investors might prefer the class B
shares (CITUB), which pay an equivalent dividend
in cash; but unlike the CITUA shares, which are con-

vertible into class B shares, CITUB shares offer no reciprocal conversion option into the class A.

RECENT DEVELOPMENTS: Wall Street credit analysts continue to accord CITUA enviable ratings on the firm's outstanding debt. Moreover, CITUA has recorded a remarkable 42 years of increased earnings-per-share (with financial ratios showing a commensurate record of improvement)—all without having added any nuclear generating capacity. Confidence for extending this performance in 1987 was fortified by higher first-quarter per-share results of 30 cents, versus 26 cents last year.

FORECAST: The Zacks' Consensus forecast for CITUA's average annual earnings-per-share increase over the next five years is not available.

Company Name: **CLAIRE'S STORES, INC.**
Listing: **(NYSE) CLE**
Type of Stock: **Retailing; Narrowly Followed; Low Price**
Z-Score: **66.7**

PROFILE: Claire's Stores, Inc. is the nation's largest costume-jewelry retailer, with revenues for the fiscal year ended January 31, 1987, of $87.2 million and earnings-per-share of $0.27. As of September 4, 1987, the range of CLE's price during the previous twelve months was:

• High: 13¼   • Low: 5

CLE's price as of the close of the first week in September was 8½.

• P/E ratio: 20   • Dividend: $0.10

RATING: Of the three brokers following Claire's Stores, Inc., one rates it a strong buy, one rates it a buy, and one rates it a hold. The average of the brokers' ratings is 1.83.

OVERVIEW AND PERSPECTIVE: Accessories, such as brooches, earrings, and handbags, and basic costume jewelry, such as occasion rings and pins, are an integral part of the women's clothing market. By retailing through its own stores, CLE management has been able to bring economies of scale to this high-profit-margin, but very fashion-conscious, business. A shift in consumer preferences, combined with an aggressive store expansion program in fiscal 1985, caused earnings to fall sharply in fiscal 1986 until management implemented several changes in operating procedures.

RECENT DEVELOPMENTS: CLE's operational style has undergone a dramatic shift. More centralized control now enables CLE to benefit not only from new, standardized store-management procedures, but also from effective inventory management aimed at maximizing the chain's growing purchasing clout with suppliers. Based on preliminary favorable indications of second quarter and first half financial results, management is confident of posting record sales and earnings for the fiscal year ending January 31, 1988.

FORECAST: Zacks' Consensus forecasts a 25.00 percent average annual earnings-per-share increase over the next five years.

Company Name: **COCA-COLA COMPANY**
Listing: **(NYSE) KO (Options on CBOE)**
Type of Stock: **Consumer Goods, nondurable;**
                        Widely Followed
Z-Score: **83.33**
   PROFILE: The Coca-Cola Company is the largest soft-drink company in the world, with 1986 per-share earnings of $1.91 on total revenues of $8.69 billion. As of September 4, 1987, the range of KO's price during the previous twelve months was:
• High: 53$^{1}/_{8}$ • Low: 32$^{7}/_{8}$
KO's price as of the close of the first week in September was 50$^{5}/_{8}$.
• P/E ratio: 19   • Dividend: $1.12

RATING: Of the eighteen brokers following KO, ten rate it a strong buy, five rate it a buy, and three rate it a hold. The average of the brokers' ratings is 1.61.

OVERVIEW AND PERSPECTIVE: Although best known for its established name brands of soft drinks, KO is an international corporation with a diverse product line. The company is organized into four sectors: the North American soft-drink business, the international soft-drink business, the entertainment business (which includes Columbia Pictures), and the foods business (which includes Minute Maid orange juice). In recent years, KO has utilized aggressive marketing, strategic acquisitions, and internal and corporate restructuring to achieve its enviable market positions in each of these business sectors.

RECENT DEVELOPMENTS: KO marked 1986, its hundredth year of business, with an innovative change in corporate structure. It reorganized a major portion of its bottling operations into a separate corporate entity, Coca-Cola Enterprises. The move is intended to enhance KO's capacity for growth and profitability.

FORECAST: Zacks' Consensus forecasts a 12.88 percent average annual earnings-per-share increase over the next five years.

Company Name: **COOPER TIRE & RUBBER COMPANY**
Listing: **(NYSE) CTB**
Type of Stock: **Consumer Goods, durable**
Z-Score: **60.00**

PROFILE: Cooper Tire & Rubber Company is the fifth-largest tire manufacturer in the U.S., with 1986 per-share earnings of $2.28 on total revenues of $578 million. As of September 4, 1987, the range of CTB's price during the previous twelve months was:

- High: 39$^3/_4$ • Low: 21$^1/_4$

CTB's price as of the close of the first week in September was 37$^5/_8$.

• P/E ratio: 14   • Dividend: $0.44

RATING: Of the five brokers following CTB, two rate it a strong buy, one rates it a buy, and two rate it a hold. The average of the brokers' ratings is 1.86.

OVERVIEW AND PERSPECTIVE: CTB has been able to operate in the highly competitive tire and rubber industry by focusing its capacity on the more stable aftermarket for tires, by exporting to some fifty countries, and by diversifying its customer base so that no one account represents more than 10 percent of sales. In recent years, management has also sought business from foreign automotive producers establishing plants in this country.

RECENT DEVELOPMENTS: Because of continued high demand, particularly for light truck and performance tires, CTB is expanding its plant capacity by about 15 percent. Strong second quarter 1987 earnings growth suggests continued earnings momentum for a company whose founder's avowed business creed of "good merchandise, fair play, and a square deal" seems to be serving it (and its customers) reasonably well over the long haul.

FORECAST: Zacks' Consensus forecasts a 7.00 percent average annual earnings-per-share increase over the next five years.

Company Name: **A. T. CROSS COMPANY**
Listing: **(ASE) ATXA**
Type of Stock: **Consumer Goods, durable**
Z-Score: **80.00**

PROFILE: A. T. Cross Company is a major international manufacturer of fine writing instruments, quality luggage, leather goods, and other distinctive gifts, with 1986 per-share earnings of $1.29 on total revenues of $155 million. As of September 4, 1987,

the range of ATXA's price during the previous twelve months was:
- High: 38^5/$_8$
- Low: 19^7/$_8$

ATXA's price as of the close of the first week in September was 34^1/$_4$.
- P/E ratio: 23
- Dividend: $0.90

RATING: Of the five brokers following ATXA, three rate it as a strong buy, one rates it a buy, and one rates it a hold. The average of the brokers' ratings is 1.60.

OVERVIEW AND PERSPECTIVE: ATXA's writing instruments historically have been priced at the prestigious quality-gift or recognition-award level. Thus, distribution through the appropriate premier retail outlets, as well as the business gift market, has been important in minimizing cyclicity. Growing international revenues now account for some 20 percent of total company revenues.

RECENT DEVELOPMENTS: ATXA's purchase several years ago of Mark Cross, a leather goods manufacturer, has begun to make profit contributions, and its compatibility with ATXA's main product line may provide new marketing opportunities. This year ATXA, in a move to expand market share, introduced a new pen-product line, "Gray by Cross." A recent acquisition, Manetti Farrow, a fashion accessories manufacturer, further suggests that ATXA is looking to boost sales by cross-selling among its expanding array of consumer wares.

FORECAST: Zacks' Consensus forecasts a 13.33 percent average annual earnings-per-share increase over the next five years.

Company Name: **DEAN FOODS COMPANY**
Listing: **(NYSE) DF**
Type of Stock: **Consumer Goods, nondurable**
Z-Score: **87.50**

PROFILE: Dean Foods Company is a major producer and distributor of food products, primarily dairy items, with fiscal May 1987 per-share earnings of $1.53 on total revenues of $1.27 billion. As of September 4, 1987, the range of DF's price during the previous twelve months was:

• High: 38½   • Low: 25⅛

DF's price as of the close of the first week in September was 35⅞.

• P/E ratio: 23   • Dividend: $0.54

RATING: Of the eight brokers following DF, two rate it a strong buy, five rate it a buy, and one rates it a hold. The average of the brokers' ratings is 1.85.

OVERVIEW AND PERSPECTIVE: Through acquisitions over the years, DF has diversified its original fluid milk-products business into such related dairy products as ice cream, cheese, and powdered creamers, as well as into canned and frozen vegetables and specialty items, such as pickles, relishes, salad dressings, sauces, puddings, juices, and chip dips. Dean Foods also operates trucking companies and franchises ice cream stores.

RECENT DEVELOPMENTS: DF announced an agreement to acquire Fairmont Products, a Belleville, Pennsylvania-based processor of dairy products, with annual sales of $30 million.

FORECAST: Zacks' Consensus forecasts a 14.07 percent average annual earnings-per-share increase over the next five years.

Company Name: **DIAGNOSTIC PRODUCTS CORPORATION**

Listing: **(NASDAQ) DPCZ**

Type of Stock: **Health Care**

Z-Score: **60.00**

PROFILE: Diagnostic Products Corporation is the world's leading independent manufacturer of immunodiagnostic kits, with 1986 per-share earnings of $1.04 on total revenues of $29.0 million. As of September 4, 1987, the range of DPCZ's price during the previous twelve months was:

- High: 40$^{1}/_{2}$ • Low: 21$^{3}/_{4}$

DPCZ's price as of the close of the first week in September was 36$^{1}/_{2}$.

- P/E ratio: 29 • Dividend: None

RATING: Of the five brokers following DPCZ, three rate it as a strong buy and two rate it as a hold. The average of the brokers' ratings is 1.80.

OVERVIEW AND PERSPECTIVE: DPCZ was formed in 1971 to develop proprietary diagnostic products for the specialty medical field of immunology, the study of immunity. DPCZ's products can be used to test for pregnancy, infertility, disease, or drug use. The company's ongoing commitment to research and development (typically about 15 percent of revenues) has given it the broadest immunodiagnostic product line in the world.

RECENT DEVELOPMENTS: In addition to the introduction of several new drug testing and diagnostic test kits, 1986 saw the start-up of DPCZ's new European Research Institute, which will initially concentrate on innovations in drug testing. Earnings for the first half of 1987 are up almost 43 percent over the first half of 1986.

FORECAST: Zacks' Consensus forecasts a 25.00 percent average annual earnings-per-share increase over the next five years.

Company Name: **DUNKIN' DONUTS INC.**
Listing: **(NASDAQ) DUNK**
Type of Stock: **Retailing; Consumer Goods,**
nondurable
Z-Score: **75.00**
PROFILE: Dunkin' Donuts Inc. is the largest operator of retail coffee and doughnut shops in the U.S.,

with fiscal October 1986 per-share earnings of $1.63 on total revenues of $104 million. As of September 4, 1987, the range of DUNK's price during the previous twelve months was:

- High: 35$^7/_8$
- Low: 26

DUNK's price as of the close of the first week of September was 26$^3/_4$.

- P/E ratio: 16
- Dividend: $0.32

RATING: Of the four brokers following DUNK, two rate it a strong buy, one rates it a buy, and one rates it a hold. The average of the brokers' ratings is 1.65.

OVERVIEW AND PERSPECTIVE: Founded in 1950 with one store in Quincy, Massachusetts, DUNK has expanded into an international chain of more than 1,600 company-owned and franchise-operated stores. From fresh coffee and a wide range of doughnut products, the menu has been expanded to include an equally wide range of pastries and croissants, hot soups, and croissant sandwiches.

RECENT DEVELOPMENTS: In fiscal 1986, the Pepsi-Cola line of beverages was added to the menu, while an agreement was reached for the company to become the exclusive licensee for Chili's Grill & Bar restaurants. The latter's wide-ranging products include baby back ribs, hamburgers, chicken sandwiches, tacos, and chili. Earnings for the six months ended April 30, 1987, were 15 cents a share, compared to 13 cents in the comparable year-earlier period; and worldwide sales totaled $345 million, versus $314 million for the prior six months.

FORECAST: Zacks' Consensus forecasts a 15.00 percent average annual earnings-per-share increase over the next five years.

Company Name: **ELAN CORPORATION, PLC**
(Public Limited Company)

Listing: (NASDAQ) ELANY (American Depository
Receipts)
Type of Stock: Health Care; High Technology;
Foreign; Narrowly Followed
Z-Score: 100.00

PROFILE: Elan Corporation, PLC is an Irish
company engaged in the licensing of pharmaceutical
delivery systems, with 1986 per-ADR earnings
equivalent to $0.19 (0.15 Irish pounds) on total reve-
nues equivalent to $7.54 million (5.83 million Irish
pounds). As of September 4, 1987, the range of
ELANY's price during the previous twelve months
was:

• High: 23   • Low: 5

ELANY's price as of the close of the first week in
September was 20³/₄.

• P/E ratio: N/A   • Dividend: NMF

RATING: Of the three brokers following ELANY,
two rate it a strong buy and one rates it a buy. The
average of the brokers' ratings is 1.33.

OVERVIEW AND PERSPECTIVE: ELANY,
based in Ireland with a U.S. subsidiary in Georgia,
produces advanced drug absorption and delivery
technologies, which it licenses to other major pharmaceutical manufacturers.

RECENT DEVELOPMENTS: In 1986, ELANY
secured fourteen new licensing contracts for its technologies and continued to pursue marketing opportunities for joint-venture drug products. A new
tablet formulation for insoluble drugs may allow
ELANY to apply its processes to drugs formerly
viewed as unable to benefit from advanced absorption technology.

FORECAST: Zacks' Consensus forecasts a 50.00
percent average annual earnings-per-ADR increase
over the next five years.

Company Name: **ELDON INDUSTRIES, INC.**
Listing: **(NYSE) ELD**
Type of Stock: **Business and Industrial**
                  Equipment; Narrowly Followed
Z-Score: **66.67**

PROFILE: Eldon Industries, Inc. is a supplier of office products and production tools for the electronics industry, with 1986 per-share earnings of $0.90 on total revenues of $72.8 million. As of September 4, 1987, the range of ELD's price during the previous twelve months was:

• High: 22³/₈   • Low: 11⁵/₈

ELD's price as of the close of the first week in September was 21.

• P/E ratio: 21   • Dividend: $0.20

RATING: Of the three brokers following ELD, two rate it a strong buy and one rates it a hold. The average of the brokers' ratings is 1.50.

OVERVIEW AND PERSPECTIVE: ELD's resources have been concentrated during the past sixteen years on new applications and selected product-line acquisitions for the office products market. These include storage, handling, and retrieval systems, computer-related media, information boards, building directories, architectural signage, and conference room furniture, such as cabinets, credenzas, and lecterns. Electronic production products involve sophisticated equipment for the assembly and repair of electronic circuits.

RECENT DEVELOPMENTS: ELD continues to focus on overseas expansion, using acquisitions to gain not only new products but also market presence in areas where expansion is a priority. Management projects strong earnings growth throughout 1987, fueled by continued new-product introductions.

FORECAST: Zacks' Consensus forecasts a 16.00 percent average annual earnings-per-share increase over the next five years.

Company Name: **EMHART CORPORATION**
Listing: **(NYSE) EMH**
Type of Stock: **Business and Industrial Equipment; Consumer Goods, durable; High Yield**
Z-Score: **75.00**

PROFILE: Emhart Corporation manufactures industrial and consumer products and information and electronic systems with 1986 per-share earnings of $2.79 on total revenues of $2.09 billion. As of September 4, 1987, the range of EMH's price during the previous twelve months was:

• High: 52$^5/8$ • Low: 30$^3/4$

EMH's price as of the close of the first week in September was 48$^7/8$.

• P/E ratio: 17   • Dividend: $1.60

RATING: Of the four brokers following EMH, two rate it a strong buy, one rates it a buy, and one rates it a hold. The average of the brokers' ratings is 1.63.

OVERVIEW AND PERSPECTIVE: An old-line supplier of fasteners and hardware products, EMH has sought to broaden earnings power over the years through a series of large-scale acquisitions. These have focused on depressed, cyclical companies in which Emhart's management expertise in low-cost manufacturing, procurement, and financial policies could effect turnarounds. In 1986, it sold its large USM shoe machinery operation and acquired Planning Research Corporation. The latter, which is engaged in information management systems, is a new market for EMH. As a result, management has embarked on a restructuring program to reposition itself into three large groups: industrial products, consumer products, and information management.

RECENT DEVELOPMENTS: Management indicated that it has identified eighteen units that do not fit in with strategic plans announced in 1986. While only five have been sold to date, the company remains confident that the remainder will be divested by the year's end.

FORECAST: Zacks' Consensus forecasts an 11.50 percent average annual earnings-per-share increase over the next five years.

Company Name: **FEDERAL EXPRESS CORPORATION**

Listing: **(NYSE) FDX (Options on CBOE)**

Type of Stock: **Business and Industrial Services; Consumer Services; Widely Followed**

Z-Score: **73.33**

PROFILE: Federal Express Corporation is one of the largest companies offering express delivery of packages and documents door-to-door throughout the United States and 85 other countries, with May 1987 per-share earnings of $2.64 on total revenues of $2.60 billion. As of September 4, 1987, the range of FDX's price during the previous twelve months was:
• High: 73³/₄   • Low: 51¹/₂
FDX's price as of the close of the first week in September was 63⁵/₈.
• P/E ratio: 20   • Dividend: None

RATING: Of the fifteen brokers following FDX, seven rate it a strong buy, four rate it a buy, and four rate it a hold. The average of the brokers' ratings is 1.80.

OVERVIEW AND PERSPECTIVE: FDX has offices in nine countries, with delivery access to 76 other countries via independent contractors. On the domestic scene, FDX provides direct overnight package delivery, available to 98 percent of the population. Employing a state-of-the-art tracking system, FDX now offers a full refund when a complete status report is not provided within thirty minutes of a customer inquiry. To maintain such a level of service, FDX operates a fleet of vans and jet aircraft as well as a sophisticated terminal in Memphis, where development of a "superhub" airport facility is underway.

RECENT DEVELOPMENTS: FDX terminated its electronic document delivery system, ZapMail, in 1987. Recent moves suggest Europe as a staging area for FDX's expansion plans, with substantially more offices and several acquisitions, including Lex Wilkinson Ltd. in 1986 and the ground operations of Williames Transport Group.

FORECAST: Zacks' Consensus forecasts an 18.20 percent average annual earnings-per-share increase over the next five years.

Company Name: **FEDERAL PAPER BOARD CO., INC.**
Listing: **(NYSE) FBO**
Type of Stock: **Industrial Products**
Z-Score: **75.00**

PROFILE: Federal Paper Board Co., Inc. is a major manufacturer of paperboard products, with 1986 per-share earnings of $1.97 on total revenues of $949 million. As of September 4, 1987, the range of FBO's price during the previous twelve months was:
• High: $51^{1}/_{2}$ • Low: $24^{1}/_{4}$
FBO's price as of the close of the first week in September was $45^{1}/_{4}$.
• P/E ratio: 15   • Dividend: $0.80

RATING: Of the eight brokers following FBO, three rate it a strong buy, three rate it a buy, and two rate it a hold. The average of the brokers' ratings is 1.88.

OVERVIEW AND PERSPECTIVE: As producer of forest products, folding cartons, recycled paperboard, and other products, FBO's sales are strengthening with the general upswing in the economy. Facilities-upgrading in recent years has positioned the company to better capitalize on commodity-pulp and bleached-paperboard product areas.

RECENT DEVELOPMENTS: In April 1987, FBO signed an agreement with Ozaki Trading Company, whereby the Japanese paper distributor will help market FBO's bleached board in Japan.

FORECAST: Zacks' Consensus forecasts a 9.80 percent average annual earnings-per-share increase over the next five years.

Company Name: **FREQUENCY ELECTRONICS, INC.**

Listing: **(ASE) FEI**

Type of Stock: **Business and Industrial Equipment; High Technology; Narrowly Followed**

Z-Score: **66.67**

PROFILE: Frequency Electronics, Inc. manufactures specialized microwave products and instruments, with fiscal April 1987 per-share earnings of $0.96 on total revenues of $36.0 million. As of September 4, 1987, the range of FEI's price during the previous twelve months was:

• High: $29^1/_2$ • Low: $19^1/_8$

FEI's price as of the close of the first week in September was $22^3/_8$.

• P/E ratio: 23   • Dividend: None

RATING: Of the three brokers following FEI, two rate it a strong buy and one rates it a hold. The average of the brokers' ratings is 1.67.

OVERVIEW AND PERSPECTIVE: FEI's initial product line was the quartz crystal filters used in communications products, specifically microwave and radar systems, to separate interference from the primary signal. Over the years, this activity evolved through internal development and acquisitions into making components and related hardware, as well as the necessary test and measurement instrumentation.

RECENT DEVELOPMENTS: Management recently announced an agreement with TRW Inc. to acquire its TRW Microwave Inc. subsidiary. This operation makes microwave subsystems and components for many of the markets served by FEI.

FORECAST: Zacks' Consensus forecasts a 27.50 percent average annual earnings-per-share increase over the next five years.

Company Name: **GANTOS, INC.**
Listing: (NASDAQ) GNTS
Type of Stock: Retailing
Z-Score: 80.00

PROFILE: Gantos, Inc. is a retailer specializing in women's fashion apparel and accessories, with fiscal 1986 (ended January 1987) per-share earnings of $0.90 on total revenues of $98.4 million. As of September 4, 1987, the range of GNTS's price during the previous twelve months was:

• High: $23^3/_8$ • Low: $13^1/_2$

GNTS's price as of the close of the first week in September was $19^3/_4$.

• P/E ratio: 21   • Dividend: None

RATING: Of the five brokers following GNTS, two rate it a strong buy, two rate it a buy, and one rates it a hold. The average of the brokers' ratings is 1.74.

OVERVIEW AND PERSPECTIVE: GNTS began as a family business in 1932. Since that time, Grand Rapids (Michigan)-based GNTS has grown to a chain of 67 stores throughout the Midwest and Northeast. GNTS targets the upper-middle and higher-income women's market by locating its stores in regional malls that feature one or more upscale department stores. Fashion catalogues and four Bargain Boutiques enhance GNTS's marketing and turnover of merchandise. GNTS marked its steady growth by becoming a public company in May 1986.

RECENT DEVELOPMENTS: GNTS has begun implementing its plan to expand to 200 stores by the early 1990s with the completion of a new office complex/distribution center and development of a new prototype store. During 1986, GNTS opened fifteen new stores. Net sales were up 31 percent, compared to the previous year, and net income increased 46 percent.

FORECAST: Zacks' Consensus forecasts a 25.00 percent average annual earnings-per-share increase over the next five years.

Company Name: **GREAT WESTERN FINANCIAL CORPORATION**

Listing: **(NYSE) GWF (Options on CBOE)**

Type of Stock: **Financial; Widely Followed; High Yield; Low P/E**

Z-Score: **81.25**

PROFILE: Great Western Financial Corporation is a California savings and loan holding company, with 1986 per-share earnings of $2.81 on total revenues of $3.77 billion. As of September 4, 1987, the range of GWF's price during the previous twelve months was:

• High: 24³⁄₈   • Low: 15

GWF's price as of the close of the first week of September was 21.

• P/E ratio: 8   • Dividend: $0.72

RATING: Of the sixteen brokers following GWF, eleven rate it a strong buy, two rate it a buy, and three rate it a hold. The average of the brokers' ratings is 1.50.

OVERVIEW AND PERSPECTIVE: The principal subsidiary of GWF is Great Western Savings, which serves the state of California and is the third-largest savings and loan association in the U.S. Through acquisitions made outside the state, GWF is engaged in consumer finance as well as real estate brokerage, insurance, and leasing.

RECENT DEVELOPMENTS: A 1986 acquisition brought GWF into the savings and loan market in Florida, and in 1987 GWF took over an Arizona thrift institution. Meanwhile, GWF continues to reduce its presence in insurance and leasing.

FORECAST: Zacks' Consensus forecasts a 13.44 percent average annual earnings-per-share increase over the next five years.

Company Name: **HEALTHCARE PROPERTY INVESTORS, INC.**
Listing: **(NYSE) HCP**
Type of Stock: **Health Care; Financial; High Yield**
Z-Score: **75.00**

PROFILE: HealthCare Property Investors, Inc. is a real estate investment company specializing in health-care-related properties, with 1986 per-share earnings of $1.79 on total revenues of $28.8 million. As of September 4, 1987, the range of HCP's price during the previous twelve months was:
• High: 31$3/8$ • Low: 25
HCP's price as of the close of the first week in September was 26$3/4$.
• P/E ratio: 47   • Dividend: $2.44

RATING: Of the four brokers following HCP, two rate it a strong buy, one rates it a buy, and one rates it a hold. The average of the brokers' ratings is 1.75.

OVERVIEW AND PERSPECTIVE: Organized in early 1985, HCP specializes in the ownership and development of health-care-related real estate throughout the U.S. It owns an interest in 93 properties, including 87 long-term care facilities. This interest ranges from total ownership to a 50-percent equity position. HCP does not operate any of the properties.

RECENT DEVELOPMENTS: Management said it reached an agreement to develop a $15 million free-standing comprehensive rehabilitation hospital in San Antonio, Texas. With construction expected to be completed in early 1988, HCP will own 90 percent of the hospital's real estate.

FORECAST: Zacks' Consensus forecasts an 8.00 percent average annual earnings-per-share increase over the next five years.

Company Name: **HEALTHVEST**
Listing: **(ASE) HVT**
Type of Stock: **Health Care; Financial; High Yield; Low P/E**
Z-Score: **100.00**

PROFILE: HealthVest is a real estate investment trust specializing in health-care properties, with 1986 per-share earnings of $1.05 (total revenues not available). As of September 4, 1987, the range of HVT's price during the previous twelve months was:
• High: 23$\frac{1}{2}$ • Low: 19
HVT's price as of the close of the first week in September was 19$\frac{7}{8}$.
• P/E ratio: 11   • Dividend: $2.38

RATING: Of the four brokers following HVT, two rate it a strong buy and two rate it a buy. The average of the brokers' ratings is 1.33.

OVERVIEW AND PERSPECTIVE: Founded by Healthcare International, an operator of psychiatric, geriatric, and general health-care facilities, HVT is a REIT (real estate investment trust) specializing in ownership of such properties, many of which are operated under contract by Healthcare.

RECENT DEVELOPMENTS: In 1987, HVT increased its credit facility to $105 million, giving it more capability to finance such acquisitions as its purchase, six weeks earlier, of two Florida nursing homes for $16 million.

FORECAST: Zacks' Consensus forecasts a 6.00 percent average annual earnings-per-share increase over the next five years.

Company Name: **HEXCEL CORPORATION**
Listing: **(NYSE) HXL**
Type of Stock: **Industrial Products**
Z-Score: **100.00**

PROFILE: Hexcel Corporation is one of the world's largest producers of honeycomb core materials, with 1986 per-share earnings of $2.28 on total revenues of $290 million. As of September 4, 1987, the range of HXL's price during the previous twelve months was:

- High: $59^{1}/_{4}$
- Low: $35^{1}/_{8}$

HXL's price as of the close of the first week in September was 54.

- P/E ratio: 22
- Dividend: $0.60

RATING: Of the five brokers following HXL, two rate it a strong buy and three rate it a buy. The average of the brokers' ratings is 1.56.

OVERVIEW AND PERSPECTIVE: HXL specializes in the highly complex and precise production of structural materials, particularly composites and hexagonal metal "honeycomb" cells that are combined to form sheets or panels with a high strength-to-weight ratio. While the aerospace industry has historically been HXL's largest market, the use of honeycomb in electronics and specialty plastics has been increasing in recent years. This in turn has led to a modest dollar volume of specialty products.

RECENT DEVELOPMENTS: Reflecting a larger backlog, better prices, and the sale of the company's medical-products operation (which had small revenues and poor margins), financial results for the second half of 1987 are expected to show improvement over the favorable first-half results. In June 1987,

HXL broadened its commitment to the structural-materials market with the purchase of Knytex, a maker of reinforcement fabrics.

FORECAST: Zacks' Consensus forecasts an 18.33 percent average annual earnings-per-share increase over the next five years.

Company Name: **IMO DELAVAL**
Listing: **(NYSE) IMD**
Type of Stock: **Business and Industrial Equipment; Narrowly Followed**
Z-Score: **100.00**

PROFILE: IMO Delaval is an industrial-equipment manufacturer with 1986 per-share losses of –$1.02 (total revenues not available). As of September 4, 1987, the range of IMD's price during the previous twelve months was:
• High: 36³/₄   • Low: 13³/₈
IMD's price as of the close of the first week in September was 35¹/₄.
• P/E ratio: NMF   • Dividend: $0.56

RATING: Of the three brokers following IMD, all three rate it a strong buy. The average of the brokers' ratings is 1.00.

OVERVIEW AND PERSPECTIVE: A December 1986 spin-off from Transamerica Corp, IMD manufactures instruments, controls, and other machinery for industry and the military. Products include pumps, connectors, gearing devices, turbines, engines, switches, and measurement instruments.

RECENT DEVELOPMENTS: In August 1986, IMD completed purchase of the Baird Corporation, an instrumentation firm whose product line provides a strategic fit with IMD's offerings.

FORECAST: Zacks' Consensus forecasts a 20.00 percent average annual earnings-per-share increase over the next five years.

Company Name: **INMAC**
Listing: **(NASDAQ) INMC**
Type of Stock: **Business and Industrial**
Equipment; Industrial Products;
Narrowly Followed
Z-Score: **100.00**

PROFILE: Inmac is a direct marketer of computer and communications products, with fiscal July 1986 per-share earnings of $0.61 on total revenues of $124 million. As of September 4, 1987, the range of INMC's price during the previous twelve months was:

• High: 23³/₄   • Low: 13¹/₄

INMC's price as of the close of the first week in September was 23¹/₂.

• P/E ratio: 31   • Dividend: $0.04

RATING: Of the three brokers following INMC, one rates it a strong buy and two rate it a buy. The average of the brokers' ratings is 1.37.

OVERVIEW AND PERSPECTIVE: INMC sells data-processing peripherals, supplies, and accessories via direct-mail marketing to over 1.5 million prospects nationwide. About a quarter of the 2,400 items offered are manufactured by INMC, with the remainder predominantly manufactured to order.

RECENT DEVELOPMENTS: A strong commitment to overseas sales (evidenced by INMC's publishing of catalogues in three languages other than English) has paid off, with positive revenue comparisons from European operations.

FORECAST: Zacks' Consensus forecasts a 22.50 percent average annual earnings-per-share increase over the next five years.

Company Name: **INTERFACE INC.**
Listing: **(NASDAQ) IFSIA**
Type of Stock: **Business and Industrial Equipment**
Z-Score: **75.00**

PROFILE: Interface Inc. produces carpet tiles, interior fabrics, and related specialty chemicals, with 1986 per-share earnings of $1.25 on total revenues of $137 million. As of September 4, 1987, the range of IFSIA's price during the previous twelve months was:
- High: 26³/₄
- Low: 9

IFSIA's price as of the close of the first week in September was 25³/₄.
- P/E ratio: 17
- Dividend: $0.24

RATING: Of the four brokers following IFSIA, two rate it a strong buy, one rates it a buy, and one rates it a moderate sell. The average of the brokers' ratings is 1.88.

OVERVIEW AND PERSPECTIVE: After disposing of its broadloom carpet distribution business and making three acquisitions in 1986, IFSIA is now organized into three tightly related groups: carpet tiles, its basic business; chemicals, also a basic business, further enhanced by acquisitions; and a new business—interior fabrics, the largest of the three. The interior fabrics group was a key acquisition because it broadened the company's operation in product and in worldwide distribution.

RECENT DEVELOPMENTS: Second-quarter earnings results for the three months ended March 31, 1987, were 38 cents a share compared to 28 cents for the comparable period a year earlier.

FORECAST: Zacks' Consensus forecasts a 15.33 percent average annual earnings-per-share increase over the next five years.

Company Name: **INTERMEDICS, INC.**
Listing: (NYSE) ITM
Type of Stock: **Health Care; High Technology**
Z-Score: 80.00

PROFILE: Intermedics, Inc. is a manufacturer of implantable cardiac pacemakers and implantable intraocular lenses, with a fiscal October 1986 per-share loss of -$0.55 on total revenues of $178 million. As of September 4, 1987, the range of ITM's price during the previous twelve months was:

- High: $29^1/_4$
- Low: $11^1/_2$

ITM's price as of the close of the first week in September was $28^1/_8$.

- P/E ratio: 41
- Dividend: None

RATING: Of the five brokers following ITM, three rate it a strong buy, one rates it a buy, and one rates it a hold. The average of the brokers' ratings is 1.60.

OVERVIEW AND PERSPECTIVE: ITM's primary product line is a series of implantable cardiac pacemakers and related accessories. Through acquisitions, ITM's expertise was broadened to include implantable eye lenses, orthopedic and other surgical implants, dental and oral surgery biomaterials, and industrial electronic products. However, because of several lawsuits and a sharp increase in debt, management has reorganized ITM by selling its unprofitable implantable eye lens and industrial electronic product lines.

RECENT DEVELOPMENTS: ITM's Nova MR single-chamber metabolic response pacemaker was cleared for clinical trials in mid-1987; eventual FDA approval would allow the marketing of this technologically advanced product.

FORECAST: Zacks' Consensus forecasts a 20.00 percent average annual earnings-per-share increase over the next five years.

Company Name: **INTERMET CORPORATION**
Listing: **(NASDAQ) INMT**
Type of Stock: **Industrial Products**
Z-Score: **75.00**

PROFILE: Intermet Corporation produces iron and gray iron castings, with 1986 per-share earnings of $0.90 on total revenues of $295 million. As of September 4, 1987, the range of INMT's price during the previous twelve months was:

- High: 19
- Low: $4^7/_8$

INMT's price as of the close of the first week in September was $17^1/_2$.

- P/E ratio: 19
- Dividend: $0.18

RATING: Of the four brokers following INMT, two rate it a strong buy, one rates it a buy, and one rates it a moderate sell. The average of the brokers' ratings is 1.88.

OVERVIEW AND PERSPECTIVE: INMT's formable iron and gray iron castings are sold around the world to automotive producers for use in brake, engine, suspension, and power-train parts. Because of increases in market share and the continued growth in the sale of castings for nonautomotive uses, sales have increased in thirteen of the sixteen years the firm has been in existence. Since the early 1980s, sales have also benefited from a trend among automotive manufacturers and parts suppliers to close plants and obtain increasing quantities of iron castings from outside sources, particularly INMT, the major independent foundry in the U.S.

RECENT DEVELOPMENTS: INMT plans to reopen an idle foundry as part of a new joint venture with the Ford Motor Company. Also, in keeping with its strategy repositioning itself as a global vehicular-parts supplier, INMT is completing arrangements for a joint venture in Korea and an expansion in Europe in 1988.

FORECAST: Zacks' Consensus forecasts a 13.33 percent average annual earnings-per-share increase over the next five years.

Company Name: **INTERNATIONAL BUSINESS MACHINES CORP.**

Listing: (NYSE) IBM (Options on CBOE)

Type of Stock: Widely Followed; Business and Industrial Equipment; High Technology; Business and Industrial Services

Z-Score: 71.88

PROFILE: International Business Machines Corp. is the world's largest manufacturer of data processing equipment, with 1986 per-share earnings of $7.81 on total revenues of $51.3 billion. As of September 4, 1987, the range of IBM's price during the previous twelve months was:

• High: $175^7/8$ • Low: $115^3/4$

IBM's price as of the close of the first week in September was $160^3/4$.

• P/E ratio: 23 • Dividend: $4.40

RATING: Of the thirty-two brokers following IBM, thirteen rate it a strong buy, ten rate it a buy, eight rate it a hold, and one rates it a moderate sell. The average of the brokers' ratings is 1.88.

OVERVIEW AND PERSPECTIVE: Headquartered in Armonk, New York, IBM derives some 40 percent of its revenues and earnings from foreign sources that have their own marketing, research and development, and manufacturing operations. In the wake of several disappointing earnings reports, IBM has been engaged in cost-cutting and in reconfiguring its marketing direction.

RECENT DEVELOPMENTS: Although the 1987 unveiling of the much-anticipated next-generation of IBM personal computers was somewhat clouded by the unavailability of an operating system to fully utilize them, these new PCs mark a breakthrough in IBM's marketing stance. Whereas the "open" design of earlier IBM PCs enabled numerous competitors to manufacture look-alike/work-alike "clones" whose far-lower prices grabbed most of IBM's microcomputer market share, the "closed" architecture of the new IBM PCs will make them less susceptible to being cloned. Moreover, their far greater capabilities may force many present clone-users who wish to upgrade to return to the IBM fold. Meanwhile, IBM continues developments in microscopic transistor technology, supercomputers, and superconductivity.

FORECAST: Zacks' Consensus forecasts a 12.09 percent average annual earnings-per-share increase over the next five years.

Company Name: **INTERNATIONAL LEASE FINANCE CORP.**

Listing: **(NASDAQ) ILFC**

Type of Stock: **Financial; Business and Industrial Services**

Z-Score: **80.00**

PROFILE: International Lease Finance Corp. is a premier owner-lessor of commercial jet aircraft, with fiscal November 1986 per-share earnings of $1.02 on total revenues of $124 million. As of September 4, 1987, the range of ILFC's price during the previous twelve months was:

- High: $22\frac{1}{4}$ • Low: 13

ILFC's price as of the close of the first week in September was 19.

- P/E ratio: 19   • Dividend: None

RATING: Of the five brokers following ILFC, three rate it a strong buy, one rates it a buy, and one rates it a hold. The average of the brokers' ratings is 1.60.

OVERVIEW AND PERSPECTIVE: ILFC buys, sells, and leases new and used jets to airlines around the world. The firm also remarkets fleets of old equipment, serving as agent for various airlines and financial institutions.

RECENT DEVELOPMENTS: 1986 was the fourteenth successive year of increased earnings for

ILFC, in part because of the growing tendency of aircraft to be financed via leases. Operating lessors such as ILFC bought 10 percent of all new commercial aircraft in 1986; ILFC projected that by year-end 1987 the operators' aggregate share would increase by 50 percent, to 15 percent of the total production of commercial aircraft.

FORECAST: Zacks' Consensus forecasts a 19.33 percent average annual earnings-per-share increase over the next five years.

Company Name: **THE INTERPUBLIC GROUP OF COMPANIES, INC.**

Listing: **(NYSE) IPG**

Type of Stock: **Business and Industrial Services; Widely Followed**

Z-Score: 75.00

PROFILE: The Interpublic Group of Companies, Inc. is one of the world's largest advertising companies, with 1986 per-share earnings of $1.87 on total revenues of $814 million. As of September 4, 1987, the range of IPG's price during the previous twelve months was:
- High: $43^1/_2$
- Low: 25

IPG's price as of the close of the first week in September was $40^1/_2$.
- P/E ratio: 20
- Dividend: $0.68

RATING: Of the twelve brokers following IPG, five rate it a strong buy, four rate it a buy, and three rate it a hold. The average of the brokers' ratings is 1.79.

OVERVIEW AND PERSPECTIVE: Successful agency network expansion and added clients have strengthened IPG's position in this highly competitive market. With advertising services offered in 51 countries under one of three agency systems—McCann-Erickson Worldwide, Marschalk Campbell-

Ewald Worldwide, and SSC&B:Lintis—more than half of IPG's income comes from outside the U.S.

RECENT DEVELOPMENTS: Because less than half a dozen large clients provide a disproportionate share of IPG's total billings, long-term strategy involves decreasing revenue dependency on these customers by expanding in both domestic and international markets. Recent acquisitions of foreign operations will help position IPG as a likely agency of choice for the multinational advertising dollar.

FORECAST: Zacks' Consensus forecasts a 12.44 percent average annual earnings-per-share increase over the next five years.

Company Name: **J. P. INDUSTRIES, INC.**
Listing: **(NYSE) JPI**
Type of Stock: **Industrial Products; Consumer Goods, durable**
Z-Score: **66.67**

PROFILE: J. P. Industries, Inc. manufactures industrial and consumer durable products, with fiscal September 1986 per-share earnings of $1.07 on total revenues of $234 million. As of September 4, 1987, the range of JPI's price during the previous twelve months was:

• High: 24⅞   • Low: 14¾

JPI's price as of the close of the first week in September was 23.

• P/E ratio: 19   • Dividend: None

RATING: Of the six brokers following JPI, four rate it a strong buy and two rate it a hold. The average of the brokers' ratings is 1.55.

OVERVIEW AND PERSPECTIVE: JPI was formed in 1979 to develop, through the acquisition of poorly performing firms, a diversified range of manufactured products. Currently, plumbing businesses provide most of its revenues, but most of JPI's profits come from components made for the automotive, farm equipment, marine, and railroad industries. International operations are also important to profits.

RECENT DEVELOPMENTS: Growth through acquisition has been the hallmark of JPI's strategy. Early 1987 saw the completion of JPI's acquisition of an engine components operation. More recently, JPI completed a licensing agreement with Nippon Leakless Industrial Co., giving JPI the rights to produce the Japanese firm's gaskets in the U.S. These two deals alone could result in a 70 percent increase in JPI's annual sales.

FORECAST: Zacks' Consensus forecasts a 20.38 percent average annual earnings-per-share increase over the next five years.

Company Name: **KAMAN CORPORATION**
Listing: **(NASDAQ) KAMNA**
Type of Stock: **Business and Industrial Equipment; Consumer Goods, durable**
Z-Score: **71.43**

PROFILE: Kaman Corporation is a diversified supplier of products and services, principally to the aerospace industry, with 1986 per-share earnings of $1.86 on total revenues in 1986 of $588 million. As of September 4, 1987, the range of KAMNA's price during the previous twelve months was:

• High: 32   • Low: 21$^{1/4}$

KAMNA's price as of the close of the first week in September was 29$^{1/2}$.

• P/E ratio: 15   • Dividend: $0.52

RATING: Of the seven brokers following KAMNA, five rate it a strong buy and two rate it a hold. The average of the brokers' ratings is 1.50.

OVERVIEW AND PERSPECTIVE: A long-time contractor to the aerospace industry in general and the Defense Department in particular, KAMNA has focused its efforts on specialized projects and applications involving engineering and problem-solving skills. As a result, 45 percent of 1986 sales were related to contracts with the U.S. government. Timely nongovernment acquisitions—distribution of industrial products and musical instruments—have also reinforced overall growth in sales and earning through the years.

RECENT DEVELOPMENTS: Based on the receipt of several large contracts from defense-related organizations, KAMNA's backlog continues to grow. This has increased management's confidence that 1987 financial results will set all-time records.

FORECAST: Zacks' Consensus forecasts a 12.00 percent average annual earnings-per-share increase over the next five years.

Company Name: **KAYDON CORPORATION**
Listing: **(NASDAQ) KDON**
Type of Stock: **Industrial Products**
Z-Score: **66.67**

PROFILE: Kaydon Corporation produces custom-engineered bearing-related products, with 1986 per-share earnings of $1.19 on total revenues of $113 million. As of September 4, 1987, the range of KDON's price during the previous twelve months was:

• High: 34   • Low: 7

KDON's price as of the close of the first week in September was 31.

• P/E ratio: 19   • Dividend: $0.10

RATING: Of the three brokers following KDON, two rate it a strong buy and one rates it a hold. The average of the brokers' ratings is 1.67.

OVERVIEW AND PERSPECTIVE: KDON, spun off from Bairnco Corp. in 1984, has reacted to the substantial international competition for bearing-related applications by focusing on the specialty or high-engineering needs of the aerospace, construction, and energy industries while reducing its presence in the more price-sensitive automotive and agricultural equipment markets. The company also has sought to broaden its custom-engineered strategy through acquisitions—last year it bought Koppers Co.'s Ring and Seal division—whose customer bases can provide opportunities for crossselling other KDON products.

RECENT DEVELOPMENTS: KDON announced an agreement to buy the Spirolox product line of specialty locking rings from TRW Inc. for $5.1 million in cash.

FORECAST: Zacks' Consensus forecasts a 12.00 percent average annual earnings-per-share increase over the next five years.

Company Name: **KEMPER CORP.**
Listing: **(NASDAQ) KEMC**
Type of Stock: **Financial; Widely Followed; Low P/E**
Z-Score: **69.23**

PROFILE: Kemper Corp. is the investor-owned portion of the Kemper Group, with interests in virtually all types of insurance, financial, and related businesses, with 1986 per-share earnings of $2.51 on total revenues of $3.33 billion. As of September 4, 1987, the range of KEMC's price during the previous twelve months was:

- High: 38³/₄   • Low: 23¹/₄

KEMC's price as of the close of the first week in September was 31⁵/₈.

- P/E ratio: 10   • Dividend: $0.60

RATING: Of the thirteen brokers following KEMC, five rate it a strong buy, four rate it a buy, and four rate it a hold. The average of the brokers' ratings is 1.87.

OVERVIEW AND PERSPECTIVE: Over the years, KEMC, once predominantly a property-casualty insurance holding company, has, through internal growth and acquisition, expanded its position in life insurance and financial services to the point where these now constitute the majority of premium income and fees.

RECENT DEVELOPMENTS: In July 1987, KEMC agreed to sell certain of its health and accident insurance operations, as well as other disability insurance operations. Earnings for the first half of 1987 were 68 percent above those of the comparable 1986 period.

FORECAST: Zacks' Consensus forecasts an 11.25 percent average annual earnings-per-share increase over the next five years.

Company Name: **KLLM TRANSPORT SERVICES, INC.**

Listing: **(NASDAQ) KLLM**

Type of Stock: **Business and Industrial Services; Narrowly Followed**

Z-Score: **66.67**

PROFILE: KLLM Transport Services, Inc. is an irregular-route trucking company, with 1986 per-share earnings of $1.15 (1986 revenues unavailable; 1985 total revenues were $46.9 million). As of September 4, 1987, the range of KLLM's price during the previous twelve months was:

- High: $19\frac{1}{2}$
- Low: $12\frac{3}{4}$

KLLM's price as of the close of the first week in September was $16\frac{1}{2}$.

- P/E ratio: 19
- Dividend: None

RATING: Of the three brokers following KLLM, two rate it a strong buy and one rates it a hold. The average of the brokers' ratings is 1.67.

OVERVIEW AND PERSPECTIVE: KLLM is an irregular-route "truckload" shipper, one of several dozen similar transportation companies that were founded in the wake of the deregulation of the trucking industry several years ago. KLLM has facilities in Texas, Mississippi, Georgia, and New Jersey and operates more than 470 tractors and 550 trailers.

RECENT DEVELOPMENTS: Sale of 1.2 million additional common shares in mid-1986, to provide funds for balance-sheet restructuring, diluted KLLM's earnings, resulting in negative per-share earnings for the first half of 1987, in contrast to the same period in 1986. The Zacks' Consensus estimate for 1988 earnings per share, however, suggests a resumption of earnings momentum, even on a per-share basis.

FORECAST: Zacks' Consensus forecasts a 20.33 percent average annual earnings-per-share increase over the next five years.

Company Name: **KNOGO CORPORATION**
Listing: **(NYSE) KNO**
Type of Stock: **Business and Industrial Equipment; Retailing; High Technology**
Z-Score: **100.00**

PROFILE: Knogo Corporation produces electronic article-surveillance (EAS) systems that are used predominantly to detect and deter shoplifting, with fiscal February 1987 per-share earnings of $1.25 on total revenues of $49.0 million. As of September 4, 1987, the range of KNO's price during the previous twelve months was:
- High: 28⅞
- Low: 17

KNO's price as of the close of the first week in September was 21.

• P/E ratio: 16   • Dividend: $0.30

RATING: Of the four brokers following KNO, two rate it a strong buy and two rate it a buy. The average of the brokers' ratings is 1.50.

OVERVIEW AND PERSPECTIVE: KNO created the EAS (electronic article-surveillance) industry twenty years ago and has maintained a position of leadership with its proprietary technology ever since. The RF (Radio Frequency) System, originally developed by Knogo, has become the industry-standard antishoplifting technology. In 1985, Knogo introduced another major advancement with its Chameleon system. Based on micro-magnetic technology and utilizing a small wire-like target (Electro Thred) that can be installed in consumer products at the point of manufacturing, the Chameleon system for marking consumer products is both inexpensive and recyclable.

RECENT DEVELOPMENTS: Although KNO has been more successful in getting its systems into stores than shoplifters are in getting goods out of stores protected by the systems, total world market penetration for EAS systems is assessed at only 10 percent of soft goods retailing sites and only 2 percent of hard goods retailers. KNO accordingly prefers to focus on product innovations within its original field, rather than pursuing paths of diversification or acquisition. The versatility of Electro Thred is attracting a variety of new customers, and the company has been expanding its international manufacturing capabilities to meet the demand.

FORECAST: Zacks' Consensus forecasts a 22.50 percent average annual earnings-per-share increase over the next five years.

Company Name: **KOPPERS COMPANY, INC.**
Listing: **(NYSE) KOP**
Type of Stock: **Industrial Products; Energy and Natural Resources; Diversified**
Z-Score: **80.00**

PROFILE: Koppers Company, Inc. is a diversified producer of aggregates and construction materials and coal-and-wood-based chemicals, with 1986 per-share earnings of $2.09 on total revenues of $1.40 billion. As of September 4, 1987, the range of KOP's price during the previous twelve months was:
• High: 47⅞   • Low: 22
KOP's price as of the close of the first week in September was 44⅞.
• P/E ratio: 20   • Dividend: $1.20

RATING: Of the five brokers following KOP, three rate it a strong buy, one rates it a buy, and one rates it a hold. The average of the brokers' ratings is 1.60.

OVERVIEW AND PERSPECTIVE: KOP, an important supplier of specialty coke for the steel and metal processing industries, in 1984 embarked on an asset deployment and acquisition program. KOP's principal operations are now in construction materials (crushed stone, sand, gravel, and related aggregates) and in chemicals and allied products, which consist of coal-derivative products, chemically treated wood, and wood-treating chemicals.

RECENT DEVELOPMENTS: Restructuring at KOP, in progress these past five years, continues with the formation of a Civil Technology subsidiary, which will handle provision of products and services to the civil engineering and construction sectors. Improved profitability and asset divestitures also enabled KOP to cut its debt almost in half in 1986. More recently, KOP began selling kits for testing turf grass for fungal infections (marketed to golf courses) and bought Spectrix Corp., an environmental analysis firm whose activities include the testing of drinking water.

FORECAST: Zacks' Consensus forecasts an 11.00 percent average annual earnings-per-share increase over the next five years.

Company Name: **LAIDLAW TRANSPORTATION LIMITED (class B shares)**
Listing: **(NASDAQ) LDMFB**
Type of Stock: **Business and Industrial Services; Foreign; Narrowly Followed**
Z-Score: **100.00**

PROFILE: Laidlaw Transportation Limited is the largest operator of school buses in North America and also controls the continent's third-largest solid-waste services company, with fiscal August 1986 per-share earnings of $0.42 on total revenues of $718 million. As of September 4, 1987, the range of LDMFB's price during the previous twelve months was:
• High: $16^5/8$ • Low: $4^1/4$
LDMFB's price as of the close of the first week in September was $16^3/8$.
• P/E ratio: 26   • Dividend: $0.16

RATING: All three of the brokers following Laidlaw Transportation Limited rate it a buy. The average of the brokers' ratings is 1.70.

OVERVIEW AND PERSPECTIVE: Through acquisitions over the past two years, this Canadian-based leading operator of school buses in North America has now become the third-largest chemical and waste-management company in this hemisphere. This strategy was conceived in an effort to quickly diversify into two essentially noncyclical businesses with continued growth potential.

RECENT DEVELOPMENTS: Laidlaw's October 1986 acquisition of GSX added new markets and increased exposure to the chemical waste disposal business, whose higher profit margins make it a likely area of focus for the company's future growth. Laidlaw also continues to pick up more school bus business by winning new contracts and buying smaller companies. In a departure from these efforts, Laidlaw agreed to purchase Monroe Tree & Lawntender Inc., a tree-maintenance service firm with contracts from utilities and municipalities in four states.

FORECAST: Zacks' Consensus forecasts a 27.75 percent average annual earnings-per-share increase over the next five years.

Company Name: **LA PETITE ACADEMY, INC.**
Listing: **(NASDAQ) LPAI**
Type of Stock: **Consumer Services; Emerging Growth**
Z-Score: **83.33**

PROFILE: La Petite Academy, Inc. operates child-care and preschool education centers across the U.S., with 1986 per-share earnings of $0.49 on total revenues of $105 million. As of September 4, 1987 the range of LPAI's price during the previous twelve months was:
• High: 22 1/2   • Low: 7 1/2
LPAI's price as of the close of the first week in September was 20 1/2.
• P/E ratio: 36   • Dividend: None

RATING: Of the six brokers following LPAI, five rate it as a strong buy and one rates it a hold. The average of the brokers' ratings is 1.33.

OVERVIEW AND PERSPECTIVE: Spun off from CenCor, Inc. in 1983, LPAI had 537 centers in 27 states as of year-end 1986, serving over 50,000 children from six weeks to twelve years of age. About 210 centers have been opened in the past three years, including a record 85 centers in 1986, and plans call for some 90 units to be opened this year. Because the company acquires the land for a new center and constructs the facility, it relies on long-term financing techniques, including sale and operating leaseback transactions.

RECENT DEVELOPMENTS: 1986 saw LPAI moving into new marketing areas with the establishment of Montessori schools and an on-site corporate day-care center, as well as its "SuperStar Club" after-school activity program. Earnings for the second quarter ended June 30, 1987, reached 16 cents a share, compared to 12 cents for the same period the year before, while revenues rose to $32.0 million versus $25.2 million a year earlier.

FORECAST: Zacks' Consensus forecasts a 27.50 percent average annual earnings-per-share increase over the next five years.

Company Name: **LEARONAL INC.**
Listing: (NYSE) **LRI**
Type of Stock: **Industrial Products; High Technology; Business and Industrial Services**
Z-Score: **75.00**

PROFILE: LeaRonal Inc. is an applied technology/ specialty chemical firm, with fiscal 1986 (ended February 1987) per-share earnings of $1.01 on total revenues of $128 million. As of September 4, 1987, the range of LRI's price during the previous twelve months was:

- High: 22⅝   - Low: 12⅝

LRI's price as of the close of the first week in September was 21¼.

- P/E ratio: 20   - Dividend: $0.48

RATING: Of the four brokers following LRI, two rate it a strong buy, one rates it a buy, and one rates it a hold. The average of the brokers' ratings is 1.75.

OVERVIEW AND PERSPECTIVE: LRI produces materials used for manufacturing semiconductors, electronic components, and other devices. Once heavily involved in metal-plating, LRI now makes a wide variety of compounds and develops processes that it sells to companies whose products range from electronic devices to automobiles.

RECENT DEVELOPMENTS: 1986 saw LRI increase its commitment to specialty photopolymers, with new products and joint ventures with foreign and domestic firms. Continued modernization of research facilities enables LRI to develop and introduce products geared to the evolving needs of its high-tech customer base.

FORECAST: Zacks' Consensus forecasts a 15.00 percent average annual earnings-per-share increase over the next five years.

Company Name: **LEGGETT & PLATT, INC.**
Listing: **(NYSE) LEG**
Type of Stock: **Industrial Products**
Z-Score: **60.00**

PROFILE: Leggett & Platt, Inc. produces components for the bedding and furniture market, with 1986 per-share earnings of $1.93 on total revenues of $586 million. As of September 4, 1987, the range of LEG's price during the previous twelve months was:
• High: 36⅞   • Low: 24⅞
LEG's price as of the close of the first week in September was 33¾.
• P/E ratio: 15   • Dividend: $0.56

RATING: Of the five brokers following LEG, two rate it a strong buy, one rates it a buy, and two rate it a hold. The average of the brokers' ratings is 1.80.

OVERVIEW AND PERSPECTIVE: Through acquisitions, LEG has diversified its leading position as a supplier of spring assemblies for the bedding market to become a broad supplier of related components to furniture makers, as well as manufacturing its own finished furniture. In addition, its Diversified Products group has enabled Leggett & Platt to enter industrial markets.

RECENT DEVELOPMENTS: Current trends on both the supply and the demand sides of the furniture business bode favorably for LEG. As consumers' discretionary income increasingly finds its way into furniture purchases, furniture makers find greater production economies through assembly of parts made by outside manufacturers.

FORECAST: Zacks' Consensus forecasts a 15.00 percent average annual earnings-per-share increase over the next five years.

Company Name: **MANUFACTURERS NATIONAL CORPORATION**

Listing: **(NASDAQ) MNTL**
Type of Stock: **Financial**
Z-Score: **80.00**

PROFILE: Manufacturers National Corporation is a regional bank holding company, with 1986 per-share earnings of $5.27 on total revenues of $227 million. As of September 4, 1987, the range of MNTL's price during the previous twelve months was:
• High: 52½   • Low: 38
MNTL's price as of the close of the first week in September was 50½.
• P/E ratio: 16   • Dividend: $1.44

RATING: Of the five brokers following MNTL, three rate it a strong buy, one rates it a buy, and one rates it a hold. The average of the brokers' ratings is 1.60.

OVERVIEW AND PERSPECTIVE: With eleven banks and related subsidiaries, MNTL offers a broad spectrum of financial services to customers worldwide. Headquartered in Detroit, it is benefiting from the recent expansion in that region's economy, having experienced four consecutive years of record earnings. During 1986, MNTL substantially reduced its volume of nonperforming loans, completed its acquisition of a customhouse broker and freight-forwarding firm through an offering of stock, and announced the intended sale of a subsidiary bank.

RECENT DEVELOPMENTS: In June 1987, MNTL announced its intent to acquire Affiliated Bank Group, Inc. in Illinois. MNTL also plans to merge several affiliates in Michigan into its Manufacturers National Bank of Detroit.

FORECAST: Zacks' Consensus forecasts a 9.67 percent average annual earnings-per-share increase over the next five years.

Company Name: **MARRIOTT CORPORATION**
Listing: (NYSE) MHS (Options on PHL)
Type of Stock: **Consumer Services; Business and Industrial Services; Retailing; Widely Followed**

Z-Score: 76.92

PROFILE: Marriott Corporation is a diversified company concentrating in hotels and related lodging, food management services for corporate and institutional markets, and restaurants, with 1986 per-share earnings of $1.40 on total revenues of $5.27 billion. As of September 4, 1987, the range of MHS's price during the previous twelve months was:
• High: 43³/₄   • Low: 27³/₈
MHS's price as of the close of the first week in September was 37³/₄.
• P/E ratio: 28   • Dividend: $0.16

RATING: Of the thirteen brokers following MHS, six rate it a strong buy, four rate it a buy, and three rate it a hold. The average of the brokers' ratings is 1.72.

OVERVIEW AND PERSPECTIVE: Dating back to 1927, MHS has more than sixty years of experience to support its current operations and franchises in 48 states and 27 countries. In addition to its popular line of hotels, MHS has a healthy share of the contract food-service industry catering to airlines, health-care facilities, and educational institutions. Its restaurant operations include Big Boy family restaurants, Roy Rogers fast-food restaurants, and Hot Shoppes cafeterias. MHS has posted strong earnings increases each year for more than a decade.

RECENT DEVELOPMENTS: MHS acquired SAGA Corporation, a large contract food-service, in 1986. Combined with its 1985 acquisition of Howard Johnson Restaurants and the proposed purchase of Denny's family restaurants, the new buy gives MHS a solid position in both the restaurant industry and the contract food-service markets. The company intends to expand its hotel operations over the next three years and is also opening a line of moderate-priced lodgings, while continuing its highly successful strategy of developing hotel properties, then selling them to investors and managing them.

FORECAST: Zacks' Consensus forecasts a 19.25 percent average annual earnings-per-share increase over the next five years.

Company Name: **MASCO INDUSTRIES**
Listing: (NASDAQ) MASX
Type of Stock: **Industrial Products; Business and Industrial Equipment**
Z-Score: 77.78
PROFILE: Masco Industries is a diversified industrial manufacturer, with 1986 per-share earnings of $0.41 on total revenues of $712 million. As of September 4, 1987, the range of MASX's price during the previous twelve months was:

• High: 18³/₄   • Low: 9¹/₄

MASX's price as of the close of the first week in September was 16¹/₂.

• P/E ratio: 25   • Dividend: None

RATING: Of the nine brokers following MASX, five rate it a strong buy, two rate it a buy, one rates it a hold, and one rates it a moderate sell. The average of the brokers' ratings is 1.67.

OVERVIEW AND PERSPECTIVE: Spun off in 1984 from Masco Corporation (which retains a 42 percent ownership share), MASX now carries on Masco's products: custom-engineered metal products for the auto and truck industries and specialized tools and devices for the oil exploration, steel, and chemical industries.

RECENT DEVELOPMENTS: 1986 saw the acquisition of three firms engaged in the manufacture of auto parts and the reorganization of several other operations into an architectural-products group.

FORECAST: Zacks' Consensus forecasts a 20.75 percent average annual earnings-per-share increase over the next five years.

Company Name: **McDONALD'S CORPORATION**
Listing: **(NYSE) MCD (Options on CBOE)**
Type of Stock: **Retailing; Consumer Goods, nondurable; Widely Followed**
Z-Score: **88.00**

PROFILE: McDonald's Corporation is the largest fast-food service company in the world, with 1986 per-share earnings of $2.49 on total revenues of $4.24 billion. As of September 4, 1987, the range of MCD's price during the previous twelve months was:

• High: 61¹/₈   • Low: 36⁷/₈

MCD's price as of the close of the first week in September was 55.

• P/E ratio: 21   • Dividend: $0.50

RATING: Of the twenty-five brokers following MCD, twelve rate it a strong buy, ten rate it a buy, and three rate it a hold. The average of the brokers' ratings is 1.59.

OVERVIEW AND PERSPECTIVE: MCD currently has 9,400 McDonald's restaurants in 45 countries. Although the original menu was limited, MCD's restaurants have been expanding menu offerings in recent years, garnering a strong breakfast business and adding a popular line of salads to attract health-conscious consumers. Three-quarters of MCD's restaurants are franchises operated by local businessmen, with the remaining restaurants owned by either MCD or affiliates. MCD retains ownership or control of its real estate sites.

RECENT DEVELOPMENTS: MCD's sales were up 13 percent systemwide in 1986, with much of the growth coming from overseas, where its rapidly expanding operations posted a 34 percent increase. MCD's aggressive expansion policy targets more than 500 new restaurants to be opened each year, more than a third outside the U.S. Analysts apparently expect even stronger follow-ups for earnings: The Zacks' Consensus earnings-per-share estimates for MCD's 1987 and 1988 fiscal years ($2.91 and $3.44, respectively) suggest 16 percent and 18 percent EPS gains for these next two years.

FORECAST: Zacks' Consensus forecasts a 13.83 percent average annual earnings-per-share increase over the next five years.

Company Name: **MICHAELS STORES, INC.**
Listing: (ASE) MKE
Type of Stock: **Retailing; Low Price**
Z-Score: **100.00**
   PROFILE: Michaels Stores, Inc. is a regional chain of retail stores selling craft and decorative

products for the home, with fiscal 1986 (ended January 1987) per-share earnings of $0.35 on total revenues of $116 million. As of September 4, 1987, MKE's price during the previous twelve months was:

- High: $8^3/8$
- Low: $4^7/8$

MKE's price as of the close of the first week in September was $7^3/8$.

- P/E ratio: 19
- Dividend: None

RATING: All four of the brokers following MKE rate it a strong buy. The average of the brokers' ratings is 1.00.

OVERVIEW AND PERSPECTIVE: MKE, headquartered in Dallas, specializes in decorative-arts-and-crafts merchandise, including kits and supplies for hobbies, crafts, floral decorations, and needlework. By the end of the first quarter of 1987, MKE had 54 stores operating in twelve states.

RECENT DEVELOPMENTS: In February 1987, MKE established its own purchasing, warehousing, and distribution services. Prior to February, MKE purchased these services from a third-party vendor. Corporate control of these functions will improve cost savings, while individual stores will benefit from tailored service and support.

FORECAST: Zacks' Consensus forecasts a 37.50 percent average annual earnings-per-share increase over the next five years.

Company Name: **MINNESOTA MINING AND MANUFACTURING COMPANY**
Listing: **(NYSE) MMM (Options on CBOE)**
Type of Stock: **Business and Industrial Equipment; Industrial Products; Consumer Goods, nondurable; Health Care; High Technology; Widely Followed**

Z-Score: 72.22

PROFILE: Minnesota Mining and Manufacturing Company, best-known to the general public as 3M, is a worldwide diversified manufacturer of products and systems, with 1986 per-share earnings of $3.40 on total revenues of $8.60 billion. As of September 4, 1987, the range of MMM's price during the previous twelve months was:

- High: 83$^{1/2}$
- Low: 49$^{1/2}$

MMM's price as of the close of the first week in September was 75.

- P/E ratio: 20
- Dividend: $1.81

RATING: Of the eighteen brokers following MMM, eight rate it a strong buy, five rate it a buy, and five rate it a hold. The average of the brokers' ratings is 1.79.

OVERVIEW AND PERSPECTIVE: Through its long-established base in abrasives and adhesives, MMM is unique in its ability to produce totally new products on a worldwide basis and develop them into multimillion-dollar businesses. Very few acquisitions have been made in this process and all were minor. Although the names have varied through the decades, MMM's businesses remain divided into four groups roughly equivalent in size: industrial and consumer, electronic and information technologies, life sciences, and graphic technologies.

RECENT DEVELOPMENTS: Acquisitions and marketing agreements during 1987 underscore MMM's growing commitment to the health-care industry, where the company's proved ability to channel technological innovation into successful new products should serve it well. In a meeting with the London financial community, management said that it expects higher sales and earnings in 1987 as results continue to benefit from the weakened U.S. dollar.

FORECAST: Zacks' Consensus forecasts an 11.16 percent average annual earnings-per-share increase over the next five years.

Company Name: **NATIONAL COMMERCE BANCORPORATION**

Listing: **(NASDAQ) NCBC**

Type of Stock: **Financial; Narrowly Followed**

Z-Score: **100.00**

PROFILE: National Commerce Bancorporation is a bank holding company headquartered in Memphis, Tennessee, with 1986 per-share earnings of $1.75 on total revenues of $144 million. As of September 4, 1987, the range of NCBC's price over the previous twelve months was:

- High: 26¼
- Low: 17¼

NCBC's price as of the close of the first week in September was 25¾.

- P/E ratio: 13
- Dividend: $0.52

RATING: Of the three brokers following NCBC, two rate it a strong buy and one rates it a buy. The average of the brokers' ratings is 1.33.

OVERVIEW AND PERSPECTIVE: The National Bank of Commerce is the principal holding of NCBC. The bank is known as the business bank for the Memphis area and offers a full range of commercial and retail banking services and products to its customers. NCBC has been pursuing an aggressive strategy, opening new branches in supermarkets and making sublicensing agreements with other financial institutions. The company also owns banks in Nashville and Knoxville, a data processing service, discount brokerages, and an investment advisory. Together, the subsidiaries enable NCBC to provide a strong, integrated mix of financial services and products to its markets.

RECENT DEVELOPMENTS: NCBC's stock and bond brokerage services, Commerce Investment Corp., generated a $12.3 million increase in revenue over 1985. Favorable growth prospects for the Memphis metropolitan area auger well for NCBC, which is positioned to capitalize on financial opportunities as they arise.

FORECAST: Zacks' Consensus forecasts a 15.67 percent average annual earnings-per-share increase over the next five years.

Company Name: **NATIONAL DISTILLERS AND CHEMICAL CORPORATION**

Listing: **(NYSE) DR (Options on ASE)**

Type of Stock: **Industrial Products; Energy and Natural Resources; High Yield; Low P/E**

Z-Score: 77.78

PROFILE: National Distillers and Chemical Corporation is a major manufacturer of petrochemicals and the largest producer of polyethylene, with 1986 per-share earnings of $1.75 on total revenues of $1.73 billion. As of September 4, 1987, the range of DR's price during the previous twelve months was:
- High: $81\frac{1}{2}$ • Low: $34\frac{7}{8}$

DR's price as of the close of the first week in September was $73\frac{1}{4}$.
- P/E ratio: 12   • Dividend: $2.20

RATING: Of the nine brokers following National Distillers and Chemical Corporation, five rate it a strong buy, two rate it a buy, and two rate it a hold. The average of the brokers' ratings is 1.53.

OVERVIEW AND PERSPECTIVE: Originally a distiller of whiskey products, DR gravitated into the related processing of petrochemicals as well. Although the spirits business was substantially broadened over the years into specialty products such as rye, rum, vodka, and wines, the chemical business continued to substantially overshadow it. Thus, in the early 1980s management began a program of concentrating on chemicals and selectively disposing of parts of the original spirits operation.

RECENT DEVELOPMENTS: Following its 1986 acquisitions of Texgas and Enron Chemicals, DR proceeded to divest its liquor operations, selling its distilled-spirits business in December 1986 and its winery operation in March 1987. Developments in the first half of 1987 (beginning construction of polyethylene reactor and starting operations at a new ethylene resin plant) highlight DR's continuing evolution into an industrial chemicals producer and leading propane marketer.

FORECAST: Zacks' Consensus forecasts a 14.67 percent average annual earnings-per-share increase over the next five years.

Company Name: **OIL-DRY CORPORATION OF AMERICA**

Listing: **(NASDAQ) OILC**

Type of Stock: **Industrial Products; Consumer Goods, nondurable; Narrowly Followed**

Z-Score: 100.00

PROFILE: Oil-Dry Corporation of America is a producer of specialty absorbent mineral products, with revenues in the fiscal year ended July 31, 1986, of $52.8 million and earnings-per-share of $1.11. As of September 4, 1987, the range of OILC's price during the previous twelve months was:

• High: 29¾   • Low: 16½

OILC's price as of the close of the first week in September was 23½.

• P/E ratio: 26   • Dividend: None

RATING: Of the three brokers following OILC, one rates it a strong buy and two rate it a buy. The average of the brokers' ratings is 1.60.

OVERVIEW AND PERSPECTIVE: This 46-year-old company is a leader in developing, processing, and marketing absorbent mineral products, such as cat-box absorbents; oil, grease, and water absorbents; and liquid absorbents. Other products include binders, flowability agents, soil conditioners, fertilizer agents, and hazardous-liquid absorbents. OILC looks at the demographics of an increasingly aging, urban population and sees demand for increased tonnages of cat litter in the years to come. Its AGSORB agricultural products continue to gain market share in the face of difficult times for the farm economy.

RECENT DEVELOPMENTS: 1985 saw OILC opening a new production center for floor absorbents and cat-box absorbents. In 1986, OILC's research center, working with a specially developed synthetic cat metabolism, received patent protection for a groundbreaking development in odor-controlling cat litter.

FORECAST: Zacks' Consensus forecasts a 23.00 percent average annual earnings-per-share increase over the next five years.

Company Name: **OLSTEN CORP.**
Listing: **(ASE) OLS**
Type of Stock: **Business and Industrial Services;**
   Narrowly Followed
Z-Score: **100.00**
PROFILE: Olsten Corp. provides secretarial and health-care temporary-help services, with 1986 per-share earnings of $0.76 on total revenues of $314 million. As of September 4, 1987, the range of OLS's price during the previous twelve months was:

- High: 30¼   • Low: 13¾

OLS's price as of the close of the first week in September was 26½.

- P/E ratio: 30   • Dividend: $0.20

RATING: Of the three brokers following OLS, one rates it a strong buy and two rate it a buy. The average of the brokers' ratings is 1.67.

OVERVIEW AND PERSPECTIVE: OLS specializes in the secretarial services portion of the temporary-help industry. Through acquisitions and product development it has broadened this base to include marketing, accounting, legal, light industrial, and health care.

RECENT DEVELOPMENTS: The company has expanded rapidly by setting up franchise-like operations in which each management gets a portion of profits (although OLS retains ownership), thus enabling OLS to maximize market share in an era of rising employer utilization of temporary workers.

FORECAST: Zacks' Consensus forecasts a 20.00 percent average annual earnings-per-share increase over the next five years.

Company Name: **ONEIDA LTD.**
Listing: **(NYSE) OCQ**
Type of Stock: **Consumer Goods, durable;**
                    Narrowly Followed
Z-Score: **100.00**

PROFILE: Oneida Ltd. is the world's largest producer of stainless-steel and silver- and gold-plated flatware, with fiscal 1986 (ended January 1987) per-share earnings of $0.06 on total revenues of $267 million. As of September 4, 1987, the range of OCQ's price during the previous twelve months was:

- High: 19⅝   • Low: 7⅞

OCQ's price as of the close of the first week in September was 18¼.

• P/E ratio: NMF   • Dividend: $0.40

RATING: Of the three brokers following OCQ, one rates it a strong buy and two rate it a buy. The average of the brokers' ratings is 1.67.

OVERVIEW AND PERSPECTIVE: An old, revered name in the once-fashionable market for silver- and gold-plated tableware, OCQ and its domestic counterparts have endured both a decline for such products and an enormous growth in much less expensive metal substitutes, particularly those produced by foreign manufacturers. Demographics, though, particularly those relating to new-household formations, may spell renewed interest in OCQ's wares as baby boomers opt for the accoutrements of domesticity. To take advantage of such secular trends, new management has revamped OCQ and its product lines considerably.

RECENT DEVELOPMENTS: After reporting dismal year-end results for fiscal 1986, OCQ's first-quarter 1987 report showed recent changes paying off faster than expected, with quarterly EPS of $0.54 up 1,800 percent over the year-ago quarter on a sales increase of only 7 percent. Citing several favorable factors, incuding the effect of the declining dollar on sales of foreign competition and cost efficiencies wrought by its restructuring program, management raised the indicated quarterly dividend and said that earnings for the current fiscal year, ending January 1988, could be as high as $1.20 per share.

FORECAST: Zacks' Consensus forecasts a 12.00 percent average annual earnings-per-share increase over the next five years.

Company Name: PCS, Inc.
Listing: (NASDAQ) PCSI
Type of Stock: **Health Care; Financial; Narrowly Followed; Emerging Growth**

Z-Score: **100.00**

PROFILE: PCS Inc. is a health-care payment system, with fiscal March 1987 per-share earnings of $0.53 on total revenues of $54.5 million. As of September 4, 1987, the range of PCSI's price during the previous twelve months was:

• High: 32½   • Low: 13

PCSI's price as of the close of the first week in September was 32½.

• P/E ratio: 54   • Dividend: None

RATING: Of the three brokers following PCSI, one rates it a strong buy and two rate it a buy. The average of the brokers' ratings is 1.60.

OVERVIEW AND PERSPECTIVE: Founded eighteen years ago, PCSI (whose initials stand for Pharmaceutical Card System) is the largest third-party prescription-drug claim processor in the U.S. Insurance companies, health maintenance organizations, preferred provider organizations, unions, welfare funds, and employers with self-administered health-care plans find PCSI's card system a convenient means of providing medications to those they cover as well as an economical and efficient system for health-care cost processing.

RECENT DEVELOPMENTS: PCSI's new Recap card, which utilizes state-of-the-art magnetic-strip card-reading technology, will enable PCSI to offer immediate claim-eligibility verification for transactions while the customer is waiting for the prescription to be prepared. This capability should help PCSI meet the specialized requirements of varied insurance and benefit plans.

FORECAST: Zacks' Consensus forecasts a 35.00 percent average annual earnings-per-share increase over the next five years.

Company Name: **PEGASUS GOLD INC.**
Listing: **(NASDAQ) PGULF**

Type of Stock: **Energy and Natural Resources;**
Foreign

Z-Score: **100.00**

PROFILE: Pegasus Gold Inc. mines gold and precious metals principally in the western U.S., with 1986 per-share earnings of $0.32 on total revenues of $35.1 million. As of September 4, 1987, the range of PGULF's price during the previous twelve months was:

• High: 26³/₄   • Low: 6³/₈

PGULF's price as of the close of the first week in September was 22³/₄.

• P/E ratio: 42   • Dividend: None

RATING: Of the four brokers following PGULF, three rate it a strong buy and one rates it a buy. The average of the brokers' ratings is 1.25.

OVERVIEW AND PERSPECTIVE: Headquartered in British Columbia, Canada, PGULF's mining operations are conducted principally in Montana and Nevada. Although many types of precious metals are recovered in the mining process, the primary contributor to financial results to date has been sales of gold. As recently as 1984, PGULF was a one-mine operation, but it has found that its ability to viably operate lower-grade properties makes low-cost acquisition of marginal operations the most effective use of its resources. Management has engaged in an exploration and acquisition program that is expected to bear results in 1987 and afterward.

RECENT DEVELOPMENTS: In the first eight months of 1987, PGULF, in addition to starting up mining operations at its Montana Tunnels Mine, announced the acquisition of one mining company, the leasing of another firm's Nevada claims, and a joint mining venture with a California firm.

FORECAST: Zacks' Consensus forecasts a 38.00 percent average annual earnings-per-share increase over the next five years.

Company Name: **PENNWALT CORP.**
Listing: **(NYSE) PSM**
Type of Stock: **Diversified; Industrial Products;**
Health Care; Business and
Industrial Equipment; High Yield
Z-Score: **62.50**

PROFILE: Pennwalt Corp. operates in three business lines—chemicals, health products, and business and industrial equipment—with 1986 per-share earnings of $3.64 on total revenues of $1.11 billion. As of September 4, 1987, the range of PSM's price during the previous twelve months was:

• High: 68$^{1}/_{4}$ • Low: 44

PSM's price as of the close of the first week in September was 62$^{3}/_{4}$.

• P/E ratio: 16   • Dividend: $2.40

RATING: Of the eight brokers following PSM, five rate it a strong buy and three rate it a hold. The average of the brokers' ratings is 1.75.

OVERVIEW AND PERSPECTIVE: PSM is a major diversified manufacturer whose evolution led it to a significant reorganization in the mid-1980s, notably involving the shuttering of an unprofitable caustic soda plant. Now configured in three major operating groups, chemicals and natural resources, pharmaceuticals, and equipment, PSM expects to reap tangible benefits from the restructuring by allocating corporate resources to areas with greater profit potential.

RECENT DEVELOPMENTS: PSM's agenda for its chemicals/resources division calls for increased focus on fluorochemicals and specialty chemicals. Heightened focus on research should result in more new products for the pharmaceutical group. PSM also plans to strengthen its commitment to its equipment group, where its market position suggests significant potential. In mid-1987, PSM bought a line of agricultural chemicals from a French company.

FORECAST: Zacks' Consensus forecasts a 12.50 percent average annual earnings-per-share increase over the next five years.

Company Name: **PENWEST LTD.**
Listing: **(NASDAQ) PENW**
Type of Stock: **Industrial Products; Narrowly Followed**
Z-Score: **100.00**

PROFILE: PENWEST Ltd. is a producer of agricultural products and chemicals, with fiscal August 1986 per-share earnings of $1.32 on total revenues of $135 million. As of September 4, 1987, the range of PENW's price during the previous twelve months was:

• High: $29^1/_2$ • Low: $7^5/_8$

PENW's price as of the close of the first week in September was $24^7/_8$.

• P/E ratio: 17   • Dividend: None

RATING: Of the three brokers following PENW, two rate it a strong buy and one rates it a buy. The average of the brokers' ratings is 1.10.

OVERVIEW AND PERSPECTIVE: Spun off from Univar Corp. in 1984, PENW is an agricultural-products firm. Reorientation of its Penick & Ford division from production of commodities to higher-margined products such as chemicals and flavorings, has benefited total revenue growth.

RECENT DEVELOPMENTS: Introduction of new products (including a nutrient supplement) and strong sales increases in potato starch are viewed as likely to have positive effect on future earnings.

FORECAST: Zacks' Consensus forecasts a 15.00 percent average annual earnings-per-share increase over the next five years.

Company Name: **THE PEP BOYS—MANNY,
MOE & JACK**
Listing: **(NYSE) PBY**
Type of Stock: **Retailing; Consumer Services**
Z-Score: **75.00**

PROFILE: The Pep Boys—Manny, Moe & Jack is a major operator and franchiser of discount automotive supermarkets and related repair services, with fiscal 1986 (ended January 1987) per-share earnings of $0.52 on total revenues of $486 million. As of September 4, 1987, the range of PBY's price during the previous twelve months was:

• High: 18⅞   • Low: 11¾

PBY's price as of the close of the first week in September was 17½.

• P/E ratio: 32   • Dividend: None

RATING: Of the four brokers following PBY, one rates it a strong buy, two rate it a buy, and one rates it a hold. The average of the brokers' ratings is 1.88.

OVERVIEW AND PERSPECTIVE: Established in 1921, PBY has operations unique in the marketing of automotive aftermarket parts and accessories: A complete line of products and prices is offered, in a superstore setting, for both the do-it-yourself buyer and those desiring installation. Customers are serviced through accompanying repair service bays and, more recently, seven-day-a-week service hours.

RECENT DEVELOPMENTS: In a major expansion program, management announced its intention to double the current 177 company-owned and franchised outlets in the next five years. Thirty-five stores are projected to be opened in fiscal 1987. The emphasis is on the Southwest and Southeast, with Dallas and Atlanta serving as hubs for PBY's expansion.

FORECAST: Zacks' Consensus forecasts a 21.33 percent average annual earnings-per-share increase over the next five years.

Company Name: **PEPSICO INC.**
Listing: **(NYSE) PEP (Options on CBOE)**
Type of Stock: **Consumer Goods, nondurable;**
                Widely Followed
Z-Score: 89.47

PROFILE: PepsiCo Inc. is the second-largest soft-drink producer as well as a leading snack-food maker, with 1986 per-share earnings of $1.78 on total revenues of $9.29 billion. As of September 4, 1987, the range of PEP's price during the previous twelve months was:

- High: 42$1/4$
- Low: 24$1/2$

PEP's price as of the close of the first week in September was 38.

- P/E ratio: 19
- Dividend: $0.68

RATING: Of the nineteen brokers following PEP, thirteen rate it a strong buy, four rate it a buy, and two rate it a hold. The average of the brokers' ratings is 1.42.

OVERVIEW AND PERSPECTIVE: PEP's interests lie in soft drinks (under the brands of Pepsi-Cola, Diet Pepsi, and Slice) as well as snack foods (Frito-Lay) and fast-food restaurants, including more than 6,000 Pizza Hut and Taco Bell outlets. In 1985 the company divested transportation operations and Wilson Sporting Goods. Success of newcomer Slice, with 10 percent fruit juices, has prompted the company to develop new flavors in the same line.

RECENT DEVELOPMENTS: PEP has been active on the acquisition front, buying up a group of Pepsi bottlers, Seven-Up's international operations, and the Kentucky Fried Chicken fast-food chain in 1986. New products, such as Slice and Jake's (a lower-calorie cola whose favorable test-market response prompted PEP's major competitor to launch an advertising campaign aimed at dispelling notions that Jake's is a diet cola) may hold the key to PEP's future growth.

FORECAST: Zacks' Consensus forecasts a 12.86 percent average annual earnings-per-share increase over the next five years.

Company Name: **PIC 'N' SAVE CORP.**
Listing: **(NASDAQ) PICN**
Type of Stock: **Retailing**
Z-Score: **72.73**

PROFILE: Pic 'N' Save Corp. is a leading Southwest and Rocky Mountain dealer of discontinued and discounted retail goods, with 1986 per-share earnings of $1.01 on total revenues of $305 million. As of September 4, 1987, the range of PICN's price during the previous twelve months was:

• High: $29^1/_2$ • Low: $17^5/_8$

PICN's price as of the close of the first week in September was $22^3/_4$.

• P/E ratio: 21 • Dividend: None

RATING: Of the eleven brokers following PICN, seven rate it a strong buy, one rates it a buy, two rate it a hold, and one rates it a strong sell. The average of the brokers' ratings is 1.82.

OVERVIEW AND PERSPECTIVE: California-based PICN occupies a unique niche in retailing by selling manufacturers' unwanted goods at 40 to 70 percent savings—discontinued items, factory "seconds," and improperly packaged goods. With practically no other competitors within its 107-store area, high (50 percent) margins are the norm. Economic slowdowns tend to doubly benefit the firm; price-conscious consumers are more likely to shop at discount stores, and declining retail sales elsewhere result in greater availability of close-out merchandise for such vendors as PICN. The constantly-changing product mix (imagine an ongoing, institutionalized garage sale) also serves to attract repeat customers.

RECENT DEVELOPMENTS: Earnings growth was nonexistent during 1987, in part because of the going-out-of-business sale of a major California discount chain that temporarily eroded PICN's market share. Earnings-per-share momentum should resume in 1988, based on positive showings for comparable stores' sales increases, benefits from recent operational upgrades, and continuation of PICN's expansion program.

FORECAST: Zacks' Consensus forecasts a 21.25 percent average annual earnings-per-share increase over the next five years.

Company Name: **PRIME MOTOR INNS, INC.**
Listing: **(NYSE) PDQ (Options on PAC)**
Type of Stock: **Consumer Services**
Z-Score: **75.00**

PROFILE: Prime Motor Inns, Inc. is an operator of motels and restaurants, with fiscal June 1986 per-share earnings of $1.35 on total revenues of $332 million. As of September 4, 1987, the range of PDQ's price during the previous twelve months was:
• High: $46^{1/2}$ • Low: $24^{1/2}$
PDQ's price as of the close of the first week in September was $43^{1/4}$.
• P/E ratio: 25 • Dividend: $0.08

RATING: Of the four brokers following PDQ, two rate it a strong buy, one rates it a buy, and one rates it a hold. The average of the brokers' ratings is 1.75.

OVERVIEW AND PERSPECTIVE: PDQ operates motor inns on the East Coast. About 16,000 rooms are operated under such franchises as Ramada Inn, Sheraton, Howard Johnson, Hilton, Holiday Inn, and Days Inn. Catering to the corporate market, with a high proportion of total PDQ bookings under corporate accounts, lends stability to an otherwise highly seasonal revenue stream.

RECENT DEVELOPMENTS: PDQ expects to double the number of Howard Johnson franchises in the next five years, in the process selling off the remaining Johnson operations while in some cases retaining management control.

FORECAST: Zacks' Consensus forecasts a 27.80 percent average annual earnings-per-share increase over the next five years.

Company Name: **PRIMERICA CORP.**
Listing: **(NYSE) PA (Options on ASE)**
Type of Stock: **Financial; High Yield; Retailing**
Z-Score: **62.50**

PROFILE: Primerica Corp. is a diversified consumer-products and financial company, with 1986 per-share earnings of $1.65 on total revenues of $2.89 billion. As of September 4, 1987, the range of PA's price during the previous twelve months was:
• High: 53$^{1}/_{2}$ • Low: 35$^{3}/_{4}$
PA's price as of the close of the first week in September was 44.
• P/E ratio: 13   • Dividend: $1.60

RATING: Of the eight brokers following PA, four rate it a strong buy, one rates it a buy, and three rate it a hold. The average of the brokers' ratings is 1.88.

OVERVIEW AND PERSPECTIVE: After its takeover by legendary financier Gerald Tsai, Primerica (formerly known as American Can Co.), moved to divest itself of virtually all exposure to the container business (cans, bottles, and paper products) and focus instead on financial services, including mortgage banking services, mutual funds, and life insurance. PA also sells audio equipment, prerecorded music, and athletic items.

RECENT DEVELOPMENTS: PA underscored its growing financial-services orientation with its recent $750 million acquisition of Smith, Barney, Inc., a major stock brokerage and investment banking concern.

FORECAST: Zacks' Consensus forecasts a 14.50 percent average annual earnings-per-share increase over the next five years.

Company Name: **REEVES COMMUNICATIONS CORPORATION**
Listing: **(NASDAQ) RVCC**
Type of Stock: **Consumer Services; Business and Industrial Services**
Z-Score: **75.00**

PROFILE: Reeves Communications Corporation creates, develops, and produces television programming for network, cable, and independent stations, with fiscal June 1986 per-share earnings of $0.89 on total revenues of $92 million. As of September 4, 1987, the range of RVCC's price during the previous twelve months was:

- High: $13^7/_8$ • Low: $5^3/_8$

RVCC's price as of the close of the first week in September was $12^7/_8$.

- P/E ratio: 29   • Dividend: None

RATING: Of the four brokers following RVCC, three rate it a strong buy and one rates it a hold. The average of the brokers' ratings is 1.50.

OVERVIEW AND PERSPECTIVE: RVCC, originally incorporated in 1969 as Teletape Corp., grew through acquisitions during the 1970s and developed a separate division involved in international direct marketing. In 1985, the company sold most of its direct-marketing subsidiaries in the United States and Europe, preferring to focus its expertise on the entertainment business. RVCC derives revenues from new television programming and syndication of established programs.

RECENT DEVELOPMENTS: RVCC has obtained a commitment from ABC for four new television shows. It will also be releasing episodes of *Kate & Allie* for syndication in the coming year, hoping for a strong follow-up to its 1986 syndication release of *Gimme a Break*, which bolstered profits greatly. Although the market for television programming is hardly without risk, RVCC has a successful track record in new and syndicated programming.

FORECAST: Zacks' Consensus forecasts a 19.50 percent average annual earnings-per-share increase over the next five years.

Company Name: **ROPER CORPORATION**
Listing: **(NYSE) ROP**
Type of Stock: **Consumer Goods, durable;**
Narrowly Followed; Low P/E
Z-Score: **66.67**

PROFILE: Roper Corporation manufactures and distributes outdoor power equipment and kitchen appliances, with fiscal July 1986 per-share earnings of $1.63 on total revenues of $568 million. As of September 4, 1987, the range of ROP's price during the previous twelve months was:
• High: 29⅞   • Low: 14⅞
ROP's price as of the close of the first week in September was 28⅛.
• P/E ratio: 12   • Dividend: $0.48

RATING: Of the three brokers following ROP, two rate it a strong buy and one rates it a hold. The average of the brokers' ratings is 1.50.

OVERVIEW AND PERSPECTIVE: ROP has an international reputation for producing quality gas and electric kitchen ranges. The company is also one of the largest manufacturers of outdoor power equipment, with a product line that includes lawn mowers, garden and lawn tractors, and rototillers. As a diversified manufacturer of quality durable goods, ROP has had a long-standing relationship with Sears, Roebuck and Company. Serving Sears as a major supplier of both ranges and outdoor power equipment has enabled ROP to achieve manufacturing efficiencies because of consistently high-volume production runs.

RECENT DEVELOPMENTS: In 1986, ROP sold its domestic coated-metal-products operation, which had been an unprofitable division in recent years. In addition to enhancing its current product line—attested to by strong sales of its new ranges—the company will benefit from an anticipated drop in its tax rate and an improved market for durable goods.

FORECAST: Zacks' Consensus forecasts a 20.00 percent average annual earnings-per-share increase over the next five years.

Company Name: **RUSS BERRIE & COMPANY, INC.**

Listing: **(NYSE) RUS**

Type of Stock: **Retailing; Consumer Goods, nondurable**

Z-Score: 75.00

PROFILE: Russ Berrie & Company, Inc. designs and markets impulse gifts for retail stores in the United States and abroad, with 1986 per-share earnings of $2.05 on total revenues of $229 million. As of September 4, 1987, the range of RUS's price during the previous twelve months was:

- High: 45³/₄   • Low: 26³/₄

RUS's price as of the close of the first week in September was 43³/₈.

- P/E ratio: 19   • Dividend: $0.40

RATING: Of the four brokers following RUS, one rates it a strong buy, two rate it a buy, and one rates it a hold. The average of the brokers' ratings is 1.88.

OVERVIEW AND PERSPECTIVE: RUS specializes in impulse gifts—4,500 items, such as mugs, figurines, ornaments, greeting cards, and candles—which it sells to more than 90,000 retail outlets in the U.S., Canada, and overseas. Contracting virtually all of its manufacturing to Southeast-Asian concerns, RUS, well aware of the ephemeral nature of product life-cycles in its chosen market sector, concentrates on distribution, with sales staff and warehouses primed to fill customer orders promptly.

RECENT DEVELOPMENTS: The 1986 acquisition of Freelance, Inc., a former competitor in impulse gifts, will increase RUS's market share. Other recent acquisitions include the Effanbee Doll Company; Maine Line, a greeting card manufacturer; and Fluf N' Stuf Inc., a chain of gift stores. RUS has also signed a licensing agreement with the NFL for a line of league-insignia football gifts and plans to expand and upgrade its warehouse and distribution facilities.

FORECAST: Zacks' Consensus forecasts a 16.00 percent average annual earnings-per-share increase over the next five years.

Company Name: **RYKOFF-SEXTON, INC.**
Listing: **(NYSE) RYK**
Type of Stock: **Consumer Goods, nondurable**
Z-Score: **66.67**

PROFILE: Rykoff-Sexton, Inc. is a leading manufacturer of foods and related products, with fiscal May 1987 per-share earnings of $1.14 on total revenues of $1.08 billion. As of September 4, 1987, the range of RYK's price during the previous twelve months was:

• High: $32^{1/4}$ • Low: $22^{1/8}$

RYK's price as of the close of the first week in September was $28^{1/4}$.

- P/E ratio: 25   • Dividend: $0.60

RATING: Of the six brokers following RYK, four rate it a strong buy and two rate it a hold. The average of the brokers' ratings is 1.67.

OVERVIEW AND PERSPECTIVE: This old-line company, which traces its history back to 1883, is a leading producer and distributor of food and food-related products for the food-service industry. Its food products consist of salad dressings, oils and shortenings, gelatins and dessert powders, beverage bases, and canned and frozen soups. Food-related items include cleaning compounds, detergents, dispensing equipment, dishwashing machines, and various plastic and paper items. Operations were substantially expanded with the 1983 acquisition of the venerable John Sexton & Co.

RECENT DEVELOPMENTS: While the full 1987 fiscal year earnings, $1.14 a share, fell below the 1986 total of $1.24 a share, fourth-quarter earnings showed a sharp improvement, rising from 14 cents the year-earlier period to 37 cents a share, giving confidence to management that fiscal 1988 will show improvement.

FORECAST: Zacks' Consensus forecasts a 15.50 percent average annual earnings-per-share increase over the next five years.

Company Name: **SAATCHI & SAATCHI CO. PLC**
(Public Limited Company)
Listing: **(NASDAQ) SACHY** (American Depository Receipts)
Type of Stock: **Business and Industrial Services; Foreign**
Z-Score: **72.73**

PROFILE: Saatchi & Saatchi Co. PLC is the world's largest ad agency operation, with fiscal September 1986 per-ADR earnings of $1.35 on total revenues of $644 million. As of September 4, 1987, the range of SACHY's price during the previous twelve months was:

- High: $40^{1}/_{2}$ • Low: $15^{3}/_{8}$

SACHY's price as of the close of the first week in September was $32^{1}/_{2}$.

- P/E ratio: 15   • Dividend: NMF

RATING: Of the eleven brokers following SACHY, five rate it a strong buy, three rate it a buy, and three rate it a hold. The average of the brokers' ratings is 1.77.

OVERVIEW AND PERSPECTIVE: London-based SACHY has systematically built itself into the world's largest ad agency group through acquisitions around the globe, as well as through the expansion of business with existing accounts. As now constituted, U.S. operations account for some 57 percent of total revenues, followed by the U.K. at 22 percent and the balance with 21 percent. More acquisitions are planned, especially of those agencies that can complement the company's multinational accounts strategies.

RECENT DEVELOPMENTS: SACHY continues to consolidate operations from its continued acquisitions, merging formerly disparate units. Easing of regulatory controls on European television advertising should result in greater use of the medium by continental marketers and higher commission revenues. Reflecting the successful integration of the several major acquisitions of fiscal 1986, earnings-per-ADR reached $1.00 for the six-month period ended March 31, 1987, comparing favorably with the 82 cents in earnings for the comparable period a year earlier.

FORECAST: Zacks' Consensus forecasts a 17.00 percent average annual earnings-per-ADR increase over the next five years.

Company Name: **SERVICE FRACTURING**
COMPANY
Listing: **(NASDAQ) SERF**
Type of Stock: **Business and Industrial Services;**
Narrowly Followed; Low Price
Z-Score: **66.67**

PROFILE: Service Fracturing Company is in the oil-field service business, with a fiscal March 1987 per-share loss of -$1.24 on total revenues of $6.32 million. As of September 4, 1987, the range of SERF's price during the previous twelve months was:

- High: 8$^1/_4$
- Low: 2

SERF's price as of the close of the first week in September was 7$^1/_8$.

- P/E ratio: NMF
- Dividend: None

RATING: Of the three brokers following Service Fracturing Company, one rates it a strong buy, one rates it a buy, and one rates it a hold. The average of the brokers' ratings is 1.83.

OVERVIEW AND PERSPECTIVE: SERF performs a wide range of specialized services for both newly drilled oil and gas wells and older wells, aimed at increasing their production of petroleum products. Operations are largely centered in the oil drilling states of Texas and Oklahoma, with other operations in Colorado, Nebraska, and Wyoming. As with other companies tied to the domestic drilling and maintenance of oil and gas wells, SERF's financial results have reflected the severely negative conditions of the past several years.

RECENT DEVELOPMENTS: While SERF showed a loss in fiscal 1987 as well as in fiscal 1986, the 1987 operating loss was some $1 million lower, while the company's balance sheet showed improvement and long-term debt was lowered by about $675,000. With recent indications that the trend in active gas and oil rigs is turning positive, management is optimistic that overall financial resources are in place to participate in any sustained increase in drilling opportunities.

FORECAST: Zacks' Consensus forecasts a 10.00 percent average annual earnings-per-share increase over the next five years.

Company Name: **SIZZLER RESTAURANTS**
INTERNATIONAL
Listing: **(NASDAQ) SIZZ**
Type of Stock: **Consumer Services; Emerging**
Growth
Z-Score: **87.50**

PROFILE: Sizzler Restaurants International is a major steakhouse operator, with fiscal April 1987 per-share earnings of $0.80 on total revenues of $241 million. As of September 4, 1987, the range of SIZZ's price during the previous twelve months was:
• High: $23^3/4$ • Low: $8^1/4$
SIZZ's price as of the close of the first week in September was 20.
• P/E ratio: 24   • Dividend: None

RATING: Of the eight brokers following SIZZ, four rate it a strong buy, three rate it a buy, and one rates it a hold. The average of the brokers' ratings is 1.54.

OVERVIEW AND PERSPECTIVE: Sizzler restaurants are in 170 locations in 34 states, with a concentration in the West and Southwest. Franchises account for 366 other units. Featuring steak, seafood, and salad, SIZZ's restaurants concentrate on made-to-order, quick-service family dining.

RECENT DEVELOPMENTS: After acquiring Tenly Enterprises Inc., owner of a chain of Rustler Steak Houses in the Northeast, SIZZ moved to convert these units into its own format. Plans to build new restaurants and acquire units from franchisees, as well as convert Rustler units, will expand Sizzler's market presence, particularly in light of SIZZ's proven adeptness at managing menu and restaurant-design innovations.

FORECAST: Zacks' Consensus forecasts a 20.50 percent average annual earnings-per-share increase over the next five years.

Company Name: **STANADYNE, INC.**
Listing: **(NASDAQ) STNA**
Type of Stock: **Business and Industrial Equipment; Narrowly Followed**
Z-Score: **66.67**

PROFILE: Stanadyne, Inc. is a producer of specialized precision metal products and components, with 1986 per-share earnings of $2.20 on total revenues of $493 million. As of September 4, 1987, the range of STNA's price during the previous twelve months was:

- High: $52\frac{1}{2}$
- Low: $21\frac{1}{2}$

STNA's price as of the close of the first week in September was $49\frac{3}{4}$.

- P/E ratio: 21
- Dividend: $1.20

RATING: Of the three brokers following STNA, two rate it a strong buy and one rates it a hold. The average of the brokers' ratings is 1.67.

OVERVIEW AND PERSPECTIVE: STNA's precision-metal expertise has paid off in the company's pioneering development of diesel fuel injection systems and the single-handle faucet. Other products, such as valve lifters, have established STNA as a major supplier to the transportation and plumbing industries. The company is also the country's third-largest producer of cold drawn steel bars.

RECENT DEVELOPMENTS: Results for 1986 were affected by two strikes in the second half of the year that combined to reduce overall net earnings by 40 cents a share. With volume on the upswing from the strike-deflated levels of late 1986, first-half 1987 financial results have proved favorable, and management expects this trend to continue for the remainder of the year.

FORECAST: Zacks' Consensus forecasts an 11.00 percent average annual earnings-per-share increase over the next five years.

Company Name: **STANDARD-PACIFIC (Limited Partnership)**

Listing: **(NYSE) SPF**

Type of Stock: **Business and Industrial Services; Consumer Goods, durable; Industrial Products; High Yield; Low P/E**

Z-Score: **80.00**

PROFILE: Standard Pacific constructs homes in California and has operations in several other states, with 1986 per-unit earnings of $1.11 on total revenues of $311 million. As of September 4, 1987, the range of SPF's price during the previous twelve months was:

• High: 14$7/8$ • Low: 10$1/4$

SPF's price as of the close of the first week in September was 11$3/8$.

• P/E ratio: 10   • Dividend: NMF

RATING: Of the five brokers following SPF, one rates it a strong buy, three rate it a buy, and one rates it a hold. The average of the brokers' ratings is 1.86.

OVERVIEW AND PERSPECTIVE: SPF designs and constructs homes for the medium-priced market in California, its primary base, and in Washington,

Illinois, and Texas. While these account for the majority of financial results, SPF also manufactures acoustical and other types of panels that accounted for 20 percent of profits last year.

RECENT DEVELOPMENTS: In late 1986, shareholder approval of a novel restructuring proposal resulted in SPF's transformation from a corporation into a limited partnership. Since SPF no longer exists as a corporation, it doesn't pay taxes as a corporation and thus is able to pay out a higher return to unitholders. Investors attracted to SPF's high yield should keep in mind, however, that the payments unitholders receive are not dividends but rather represent a partnership share of income, gains, losses, deductions, and credits, and must be reported as such to the IRS. Furthermore, Congress—possibly irked at a private sector solution to a legislatively created problem (double taxation of corporate earnings)—is reportedly contemplating another midgame rule change, one that might bring SPF's now-stratospheric yield down to earth.

FORECAST: Zacks' Consensus forecasts a 13.13 percent average annual earnings-per-share increase over the next five years.

Company Name: **ST. JUDE MEDICAL, INC.**
Listing: **(NASDAQ) STJM**
Type of Stock: **Health Care; High Technology;**
              Narrowly Followed
Z-Score: **100.00**

PROFILE: St. Jude Medical Inc. is a leading producer of mechanical heart valves, with 1986 per-share earnings of $1.19 on total revenues of $60.5 million. As of September 4, 1987, the range of STJM's price during the previous twelve months was:

• High: 27³/₄   • Low: 9³/₈

STJM's price as of the close of the first week in September was 26¾.

- P/E ratio: 19   • Dividend: None

RATING: All of the three brokers following STJM rate it a strong buy. The average of the brokers' ratings is 1.00.

OVERVIEW AND PERSPECTIVE: STJM's principal product, a heart valve, received FDA approval for marketing in the U.S. in 1983; since then, domestic sales have made up about half of the company's revenues. The valves are marketed through independent representatives.

RECENT DEVELOPMENTS: After settling a legal dispute with pacemaker manufacturer Intermedics in 1985, St. Jude turned its attention to recouping market share, while also focusing on new research in heart valve technology.

FORECAST: Zacks' Consensus forecasts a 22.33 percent average annual earnings-per-share increase over the next five years.

Company Name: **SUN ELECTRIC CORP.**
Listing: **(NYSE) SE**
Type of Stock: **Business and Industrial Equipment; Low Price**
Z-Score: **100.00**

PROFILE: Sun Electric Corp. is a major producer of automotive test and service equipment, with fiscal October 1986 per-share earnings of $0.20 on total revenues of $177 million. As of September 4, 1987, the range of SE's price during the previous twelve months was:

- High: 16⅜   • Low: 9⅞

SE's price as of the close of the first week in September was 12⅞.

- P/E ratio: 25   • Dividend: None

RATING: Of the four brokers following SE, two rate it a strong buy and two rate it a buy. The average of the brokers' ratings is 1.50.

OVERVIEW AND PERSPECTIVE: SE has been a long-time supplier of hand-held test and service equipment for the transportation industry, primarily automobiles, both here and abroad. In recent years, an extensive line of computerized products and systems has been added. Severely competitive conditions in the overall industry, as well as the increasingly complex nature of today's automotive engines, have led to management changes in the past few years.

RECENT DEVELOPMENTS: After four years of losses, SE eked out a profit in fiscal 1986, aided by a new line of highly computerized test equipment viewed likely to establish SE as the front runner in auto-test technology.

FORECAST: Zacks' Consensus forecasts a 13.75 percent average annual earnings-per-share increase over the next five years.

Company Name: **SUPER FOOD SERVICES, INC.**
Listing: **(ASE) SFS**
Type of Stock: **Consumer Goods, nondurable**
Z-Score: **100.00**

PROFILE: Super Food Services, Inc. is the fourth-largest publicly owned wholesale food distributor in the U.S., with fiscal August 1986 per-share earnings of $1.48 on total revenues of $1.42 billion. As of September 4, 1987, the range of SFS's price during the previous twelve months was:

• High: $29^{1/8}$ • Low: $19^{1/4}$

SFS's price as of the close of the first week in September was $26^{3/4}$.

• P/E ratio: 19   • Dividend: $0.32

RATING: Of the five brokers following SFS, two rate it a strong buy and three rate it a buy. The average of the brokers' ratings is 1.50.

OVERVIEW AND PERSPECTIVE: SFS sells food and general merchandise products to small independent grocery stores in five states and provides merchandising, promotional, and administrative services. Along with low distribution costs, such services are particularly important to SFS's customers, enabling them to compete more effectively with the buying power of the usually much larger food chains.

RECENT DEVELOPMENTS: SFS continues to upgrade and expand facilities to better serve a growing customer base. Earnings-per-share for the first half ended February 28, 1987, were 70 cents a share compared to 61 cents earned in the comparable year-earlier period.

FORECAST: Zacks' Consensus forecasts a 15.00 percent average annual earnings-per-share increase over the next five years.

Company Name: **SUPERIOR INDUSTRIES**
              INTERNATIONAL, INC.
Listing: **(ASE) SUP**
Type of Stock: **Consumer Goods, durable;**
              Narrowly Followed; Low P/E
Z-Score: **66.67**

PROFILE: Superior Industries International, Inc. is a producer and marketer of automotive and recreational-vehicle products and accessories, with 1986 per-share earnings of $1.43 on total revenues of $149 million. As of September 4, 1987, the range of SUP's price during the previous twelve months was:
• High: 19³/₈   • Low: 11¹/₈
SUP's price as of the close of the first week in September was 15⁵/₈.

• P/E ratio: 11   • Dividend: $0.25

RATING: Of the three brokers following SUP, two rate it a strong buy and one rates it a hold. The average of the brokers' ratings is 1.67.

OVERVIEW AND PERSPECTIVE: Almost all of SUP's efforts are aimed at developing consumer products for the "performance" and "performance appearance" automotive-related markets. Such products are sold as original equipment or to the aftermarket. Thus, the company's major product is aluminum road wheels (80 percent of sales) sold to the "Big Three" auto manufacturers (70 percent of sales). The automakers have increasingly favored such products as profitable optional equipment, especially on their "sportier" models.

RECENT DEVELOPMENTS: Consumer and manufacturer preference for aluminum wheels bodes well for strong revenue growth. In 1987, SUP announced commencement of a program for repurchase of 4 percent of its outstanding common stock.

FORECAST: Zacks' Consensus forecasts a 12.00 percent average annual earnings-per-share increase over the next five years.

Company Name: **TGI FRIDAY'S INC.**
Listing: **(NYSE) TGI**
Type of Stock: **Retailing; Consumer Services; Low Price**
Z-Score: **66.67**

PROFILE: TGI Friday's Inc. operates and franchises two distinctive styles of restaurants, with 1986 per-share earnings of $0.08 on total revenues of $360 million. As of September 4, 1987, the range of TGI's price during the previous twelve months was:
• High: $10^3/_4$ • Low: $6^1/_2$
TGI's price as of the close of the first week in September was $8^5/_8$.

• P/E ratio: 48   • Dividend: None

RATING: Of the six brokers following TGI, three rate it as a strong buy, one rates it a buy, and two rate it a hold. The average of the brokers' ratings is 1.80.

OVERVIEW AND PERSPECTIVE: Founded in 1965, TGI operates more than 140 owned or franchised casual-theme restaurants across the U.S. and in Europe. The company believes it has the highest per-unit sales of any nationwide restaurant chain. Excessively rapid growth during the past few years resulted in poor earnings comparisons, leading management to overhaul operating procedures in the wake of market research findings that suggested increased focus on service and customer convenience. TGI operations have been decentralized, allowing individual restaurant managers to tailor their facilities to localized consumer preferences.

RECENT DEVELOPMENTS: TGI's first international unit was opened in mid-fiscal 1986. After the unprecedented loss in the fourth quarter of 1986, first-half earnings-per-share results have improved, and management expects this favorable trend to continue for the remainder of the year.

FORECAST: Zacks' Consensus forecasts a 15.00 percent average annual earnings-per-share increase over the next five years.

Company Name: **TIMES MIRROR CO.**
Listing: **(NYSE) TMC (Options on NYSE)**
Type of Stock: **Business and Industrial Services;**
          Consumer Services;
          Widely Followed
Z-Score: **66.67**
PROFILE: Times Mirror Co. is a major diversified newspaper publisher, with 1986 per-share earnings

of $2.88 on total revenues of $2.92 billion. As of September 4, 1987, the range of TMC's price during the previous twelve months was:

• High: 105⅞   • Low: 56⅞

TMC's price as of the close of the first week in September was 94.

• P/E ratio: 19   • Dividend: $1.64

RATING: Of the eighteen brokers following TMC, seven rate it a strong buy, five rate it a buy, and six rate it a hold. The average of the brokers' ratings is 1.88.

OVERVIEW AND PERSPECTIVE: Using its extensive base in newspaper publishing, TMC has evolved a widely diversified array of communications-related activities. These include information services, commercial and cable broadcasting, magazine and book publishing, newsprint, and forest products.

RECENT DEVELOPMENTS: In 1986, TMC sold the *Dallas Times Herald* and divested the bulk of its newsprint and forest-product operations as well. It also bought the *Baltimore Sun* newspapers and plans to start publication of *Sports, Inc.* magazine in early 1988.

FORECAST: Zacks' Consensus forecasts a 14.03 percent average annual earnings-per-share increase over the next five years.

Company Name: **TOLL BROTHERS**
Listing: **(NYSE) TOL**
Type of Stock: **Business and Industrial Services; Consumer Goods, durable; Low Price**
Z-Score: **75.00**

PROFILE: Toll Brothers is engaged in the construction and marketing of residential housing, with fiscal October 1986 per-share earnings of $0.35 on

total revenues of $125 million. As of September 4, 1987, the range of TOL's price during the previous twelve months was:
- High: 16½   • Low: 3⅜

TOL's price as of the close of the first week in September was 10⅝.
- P/E ratio: 24   • Dividend: None

RATING: Of the four brokers following TOL, two rate it a strong buy, one rates it a buy, and one rates it a hold. The average of the brokers' ratings is 1.75.

OVERVIEW AND PERSPECTIVE: TOL builds homes in the eastern United States, principally in Pennsylvania and New Jersey. Typically, TOL houses are single-family homes, townhouses, and condominiums targeted to the middle-and upper-income market. The company also finances its homes, originating and then reselling mortgages.

RECENT DEVELOPMENTS: First-half comparisons for 1987 vs. 1986 showed per-share earnings of $0.12 vs. $0.07, an increase of 71 percent. As of the beginning of 1987, TOL had in development or under option housing sites with a total market value of more than $1 billion.

FORECAST: Zacks' Consensus forecasts a 28.25 percent average annual earnings-per-share increase over the next five years.

Company Name: **UNION PLANTERS CORPORATION**
Listing: **(NASDAQ) UPCM**
Type of Stock: **Financial**
Z-Score: **100.00**

PROFILE: Union Planters Corporation is a bank holding company in Memphis, Tennessee, with 1986 per-share earnings of $2.42 on total revenues of $257

million. As of September 30, 1987, UPCM's price during the previous twelve months was:
- High: 40   • Low: 18

UPCM's price as of the close of the first week in September was $34^7/8$.
- P/E ratio: 15   • Dividend: $0.30

RATING: Of the four brokers following UPCM, two rate it a strong buy and two rate it a buy. The average of the brokers' ratings is 1.50.

OVERVIEW AND PERSPECTIVE: Union Planters National Bank is the principal holding of UPCM. The bank is one of the 200 largest commercial banks in the United States and, through its subsidiaries, is also a leading provider of broker/dealer services to other financial service institutions nationwide. The bank's commercial banking services are concentrated on retail and commercial customers in Tennessee and the mid-South region. In 1986, UPCM expanded operations and strengthened its market position through the acquisition of several financial institutions in the mid-South region.

RECENT DEVELOPMENTS: UPCM's acquisitions strategy has continued into 1987 with the announcement in June of its agreement to acquire CBC Bancorp. Profitability and strong capital ratios have enabled UPCM to reinstate dividend payments.

FORECAST: Zacks' Consensus forecasts a 14.00 percent average annual earnings-per-share increase over the next five years.

Company Name: **UNITED CAROLINA BANCSHARES CORPORATION**
Listing: **(NASDAQ) UCAR**
Type of Stock: **Financial; Narrowly Followed; High Yield; Low P/E**

Z-Score: **66.67**

PROFILE: United Carolina Bancshares Corporation is a regional bank holding company, with 1986 per-share earnings of $2.78 on total revenues of $184 million. As of September 4, 1987, the range of UCAR's price during the previous twelve months was:

• High: 32   • Low: 26

UCAR's price as of the close of the first week in September was 30.

• P/E ratio: 11   • Dividend: $1.04

RATING: Of the three brokers following UCAR, two rate it a strong buy and one rates it a hold. The average of the brokers' ratings is 1.67.

OVERVIEW AND PERSPECTIVE: North Carolina-based UCAR owns the United Carolina Bank and the United Carolina Bank of South Carolina, regional banks with total assets of $1.9 billion as of year-end 1986, up 18.4 percent from a year earlier. UCAR, in setting its sights on becoming the leading mid-sized banking institution in its market, has focused on quality of service as a means of achieving its goal.

RECENT DEVELOPMENTS: 1986 found UCAR adding branches and moving into South Carolina with the acquisition of Bank of Greer, since renamed United Carolina Bank of South Carolina.

FORECAST: Zacks' Consensus forecasts an 11.33 percent average annual earnings-per-share increase over the next five years.

Company Name: **URS CORPORATION**
Listing: **(NYSE) URS**
Type of Stock: **Business and Industrial Services**
Z-Score: **75.00**

PROFILE: URS Corporation is a leading world-wide supplier of engineering and architectural services, with fiscal October 1986 per-share earnings of $1.18 on total revenues of $116 million. As of September 4, 1987, the range of URS's price during the previous twelve months was:

- High: 21⁷/₈
- Low: 14³/₈

URS's price as of the close of the first week in September was 19³/₈.

- P/E ratio: 18
- Dividend: NMF

RATING: Of the four brokers following URS, two rate it a strong buy, one rates it a buy, and one rates it a hold. The average of the brokers' ratings is 1.75.

OVERVIEW AND PERSPECTIVE: URS has a long history of providing specialized engineering and architectural services for the infrastructural segment of the construction-services market: highways, bridges, and hazardous-waste, water-resource, and power systems—projects that are generally financed by local, state, and federal governments. In recent years, management has expanded this expertise into international markets, both through acquisitions and the opening of new offices.

RECENT DEVELOPMENTS: URS announced two acquisitions that will reinforce the direction it has been pursuing in its overall strategy: Mitchell Management Systems, an advanced computer modeling company, and a 51 percent interest in SKFP International, a Hong Kong architectural design firm. Recent contracts awarded to URS include several for hazardous-waste disposal sites and one for construction management of a multipurpose convention/transportation center in Atlantic City.

FORECAST: Zacks' Consensus forecasts a 14.00 percent average annual earnings-per-share increase over the next five years.

Company Name: **VALSPAR CORPORATION**
Listing: **(ASE) VAL**
Type of Stock: **Consumer Goods, nondurable;**
Industrial Products
Z-Score: **100.00**

PROFILE: Valspar Corporation is the fifth-largest supplier of paints and coatings in the U.S., with fiscal October 1986 per-share earnings of $1.25 on total revenues of $345 million. As of September 4, 1987, the range of VAL's price during the previous twelve months was:

• High: 39$\frac{1}{8}$ • Low: 17$\frac{1}{4}$

VAL's price as of the close of the first week in September was 36$\frac{7}{8}$.

• P/E ratio: 23 • Dividend: $0.32

RATING: Of the five brokers following VAL, three rate it a strong buy and two rate it a buy. The average of the brokers' ratings is 1.36.

OVERVIEW AND PERSPECTIVE: A longtime supplier of varnish and paint products to the consumer market, as well as for specialized industrial applications, VAL has been developing new products and acquiring additional ones through a program designed to broaden its overall position in the coatings industry. As a result, total sales have grown by a factor of five and earnings by a factor of seven over the past ten years.

RECENT DEVELOPMENTS: While not yet expected to begin making significant contributions to overall profitability, the consolidation of the Enterprise Paint Companies (acquired in late 1986) should give VAL a more evenly balanced product mix. VAL also recently announced an agreement with BP Chemicals to form a partnership, to be called Valspar Mebon, to manufacture and market oil-absorbent coatings and sealants in the U.S. and Canada.

FORECAST: Zacks' Consensus forecasts a 14.00 percent average annual earnings-per-share increase over the next five years.

Company Name: **VISTA CHEMICAL**
Listing: **(NYSE) VC**
Type of Stock: **Industrial Products**
Z-Score: **75.00**

PROFILE: Vista Chemical is a chemical producer with fiscal September 1986 per-share earnings of $1.73 on total revenues of $550 million. As of September 4, 1987, the range of VC's price during the previous twelve months was:
- High: 52$\frac{1}{4}$ • Low: 17

VC's price as of the close of the first week in September was: 46$\frac{1}{4}$.
- P/E ratio: 20   • Dividend: $0.05

RATING: Of the four brokers following VC, three rate it a strong buy and one rates it a hold. The average of the brokers' ratings is 1.50.

OVERVIEW AND PERSPECTIVE: Originally a branch of DuPont's Conoco petroleum division, VC was taken private in a 1984 leveraged buyout, then offered to the public in December 1986 at $17 per share. Surfactants (used in detergents and personal care products), plasticizers, and related products make up a little more than half of sales; PVC (polyvinyl chloride) polymer products account for the bulk of the remainder.

RECENT DEVELOPMENTS: Third-quarter 1987 per-share earnings of $0.82 were up 34 percent over the $0.61 reported for the corresponding period of the previous year. 1987 also saw VC initiate a quarterly dividend payment and buy back about 5 percent of its outstanding common stock.

FORECAST: Zacks' Consensus forecasts a 25.00 percent average annual earnings-per-share increase over the next five years.

GLOSSARY

After-tax return:
The return of an investment after taxes.

Appreciate:
To increase in value.

Asked price:
The price at which a security is offered for sale on an exchange or on the over-the-counter market.

Asset:
An item that has commercial value.

Asset play:
A company whose valuable assets are not reflected in the price of the company's stock.

Back up:
The reverse movement of a stock market trend.

Balance sheet:
A financial statement showing, in condensed form, a company's assets, liabilities, and capital on a given date.

Bankruptcy:
Insolvency; the inability of an individual or corporation to pay debts.

Bear:
An investor or observer who believes the stock market will decline.

Bear market:
A declining stock market.

Bell:
The audible signal that opens and closes trading on major securities exchanges.

Big board:
Informal term describing the New York Stock Exchange.

Block:
A large holding or transaction of stock; the term is usually understood to indicate at least 10,000 shares.

Blue chip:
A company with a national reputation for products or services of high quality and broad acceptance, and an ability to make money and pay dividends to its stockholders.

Board room:
A room in a broker's office, frequented by brokers and customers, where opening, high, low, and last stock prices are quoted, either by board, ticker, or individual quotation machine.

Book value:
An accounting term that represents one measure of a stock's worth. Book value is determined by adding all of a company's tangible assets, then deducting all debts and other liabilities, plus the liquidation price of any preferred stock issues. The sum is divided by the number of common stock shares outstanding; the result is the book value per common share. It should be noted that book value does not necessarily have any relation to market value.

Broker:
An agent who handles the public's orders to buy and sell securities, and who is paid a commission for the service.

Bull:
An investor or observer who believes the stock market will rise.

Bull market:
An advancing stock market.

Call:
An issuer's right to redeem shares of preferred stock before maturity, if any.

Capital gain:
Profit from the sale of a capital asset. For federal tax purposes, capital gains are either short-term (12 months or less) or long-term (more than 12 months).

Capital loss:
Loss from the sale of a capital asset.

Capital stock:
All shares, preferred and common, representing ownership of a business.

Capitalization:
The total amount of the various securities that may be issued by a corporation. These securities include not only stocks, but debentures and bonds.

Cash sale:
A stock exchange floor transaction that calls for the securities to be delivered to the buyer on the day of purchase.

Certificate:
The physical piece of paper that signifies the ownership of stock in a corporation.

Commercial paper:
Unsecured promissory notes issued by corporations.

Common stock:
Securities representing an ownership interest in a corporation. Holders of common stock assume more risk than holders of preferred stock or bondholders, but exercise greater control, and benefit more significantly from capital appreciation and dividends.

Conglomerate:
A diversified corporation that maintains interest in a variety of industries and businesses.

Consumer spending:
A statistic kept by the federal government that measures how much consumers spend each month.

Conversion ratio:
The number of common stock shares yielded by a convertible security.

Convertible:
Preferred stock that may be exchanged by the owner for common stock or another security, usually from the same company.

Convertible bond:
A security that is issued like a bond, but can convert into a particular number of common stock shares in the company that issued the bond.

Cumulative preferred:
A stock that pays dividends on the company's common stock if one or more dividends are omitted.

Current assets:
A company's assets that may be expected to be sold, consumed, or realized in cash during the normal course of business.

Current liabilities:
Money owed and payable by a company.

Current yield:
Income received, divided by the current value or cost of the security.

Deficit spending:
The amount of money a government spends beyond what it receives in taxes and other revenues.

Deflation:
A contraction of the volume of available money or credit that results in a decline of the general price level.

Discount:
The amount by which a stock or other security is sold below its par value.

Disinflation:
A slowdown in the rate of price increases; not to be confused with *deflation*, which is a decline in the prices of goods and services.

Distributions:
Dividends paid from net income and realized capital gains.

Diversification:
Spreading investments among a broad range of companies or industries.

Dividend:
The payment distributed pro rata among the shares outstanding; the amount is determined by the company's board of directors.

Dow Jones averages:
Stock indicators published by Dow Jones & Co.; based on performance of a fixed portfolio.

Earnings report:
A company's statement of earnings or losses.

Economic indicators:
A variety of measures of the economic health of business and industry as determined by the U.S. Department of Commerce.

Employee Stock Ownership Plan (ESOP):
A program that encourages employees to purchase stock in their company.

Equity:
The ownership interest possessed by a corporation's shareholders.

Ex-dividend:
Period of time between the announcement and payment of a stock dividend. Investors who purchase shares during that interval period are not entitled to the announced dividend.

Federal Reserve System:
The banking system of the federal government.

First preferred stock:
Preferred stock with a preferential claim on dividends and assets over other preferred issues and common stock.

Fiscal year:
The accounting year of a corporation.

Floor:
The trading area of the New York Stock Exchange.

Free and open market:
A market in which price freely expresses supply and demand.

Glamour stock:
Stock that has a wide following among the public and institutional investors. A glamour stock often has a higher earnings growth rate than a *blue chip stock*.

Gross National Product (GNP):
All the goods and services produced in a country in one year.

Growth stock:
Stock offered by a company with a steady record of rapid earnings growth.

Heavy market:
A stock market characterized by falling prices caused by more offers to sell than bids to buy.

Hedge:
A method by which an investor offsets the risk of one investment against another.

CONSUMER GUIDE®

Hot issue:
A newly issued stock that is in great demand.

Illiquid:
The quality of an investment that cannot be quickly converted to cash.

Inactive stock:
An infrequently traded stock.

Indexing:
Use of a statistical measure of change in value, usually to apply some standard comparison or adjustment.

Inflation:
An increase in the volume of money, and general price level. Typically measured by several key factors.

Inflation rate:
The monthly or annual rate of price increase.

Instrument:
A vehicle for investing money.

Issue:
The distribution of a company's securities, or the securities themselves.

Leverage:
The use of borrowed money in an investment.

Liabilities:
All claims against a corporation, including taxes.

Limit:
An order to buy or sell a stated amount of a security at a predetermined—or better—price.

Liquid:
The quality of an investment that can be quickly converted to cash.

Listed stock:
The stock of a company traded on a securities exchange. A registration statement and listing application describing the company issuing such stock are filed with the Securities and Exchange Commission, and with the exchange itself.

Locked in:
A situation that prevents an investor from selling a profitable security because his profit would immediately become subject to the capital gains tax.

Margin:
The amount paid by a customer who uses his broker's credit to purchase a security.

Market price:
The last reported price at which a security sold.

NASD:
Acronym for the National Association of Securities Dealers, Inc., an association of dealers and brokers in over-the-counter securities.

NASDAQ:
Acronym for the National Association of Securities Dealers Automated Quotations, an automated network that provides dealers and brokers with information about securities that are traded over the counter.

Negotiable security:
A security that can be sold or traded.

New issue:
A stock or other security sold by a corporation for the first time.

NYSE common stock index:
A composite index covering price movements of all common stocks listed on the New York Stock Exchange.

Odd lot:
A transaction of 1 to 9 shares, or 1 to 99 shares; stocks are commonly sold in lots of 10 or 100 shares.

Option:
The right to buy or sell a security within a specified time at a fixed price.

Over-the-counter market:
A securities market that is conducted by dealers throughout the country through negotiation rather than through the use of an auction system.

Paper profit:
Unrealized profit on a security that is not sold by the owner.

Par:
A dollar amount assigned by a company's charter to a share of common stock. Par value of common stock does not necessarily reflect the stock's market value.

Passed dividend:
A scheduled dividend that is omitted.

Penny stocks:
Inexpensive, highly speculative stock issues that sell for less than one dollar a share.

Point:
As pertaining to stocks, a point is equal to one dollar

Portfolio:
The securities held by an individual or institution.

Preferred stock:
Stock that has a claim on the company's earnings before payment may be made on common stock.

Premium:
The amount by which a preferred stock sells above its par value.

Price to earnings ratio:
The price of a share of stock divided by earnings per share; calculated for a 12-month period.

Principal:
The amount of money invested.

Quotation:
The highest bid to buy and the lowest offer to sell a stock at a given time.

Ratings:
Designations used by investors' services to give relative indications of stock quality.

Real rate of return:
The return on an investment after accounting for taxes and inflation.

Return:
The profit on an investment before taxes. This includes current income and growth or loss in the value of the assets. Sometimes called *total return*.

Risk:
The possibility of loss of principal or purchasing power.

Rollover:
The reinvestment of funds from one vehicle to another.

SEC:
Acronym for the Securities and Exchange Commission, a federal agency that protects investors.

Security:
A financial instrument, such as stocks and bonds, that entitles the investor to specific rights.

Share:
A unit of equity or ownership in a corporation.

Speculator:
An investor who accepts risk in hope of capital gain.

Split:
The division of a corporation's outstanding stock shares into a larger number of shares. For example, a 2-for-1 split by a company with 2 million shares outstanding results in 4 million shares outstanding.

Stock:
An ownership share in a corporation.

Stock dividend:
A dividend paid in securities instead of cash.

Switching:
The act of selling one security and buying another.

Tax base:
The total resources available for taxation.

Tax bracket:
The percentage rate at which the last dollar of income earned is taxed.

Trader:
An individual investor who buys and sells for short-term profit.

Unlisted:
A security that is not listed on a stock exchange.

Volatile:
The quality of rapid and/or extreme fluctuation in the market price of an asset.

Voting right:
The right given to stockholders to vote their stock in the affairs of the company.